From the UPANISHADS

ANANDA WOOD

First Edition 1996
Second Edition 1997
Third and Revised Edition 2009

Credits: Cover Design by Red Sky Designs, Mumbai
Book Design by Ananda Wood

Published by: ZEN PUBLICATIONS
A Division of Maoli Media Private Limited
60, Juhu Supreme Shopping Centre,
Gulmohar Cross Road No. 9,
JVPD Scheme, Juhu,
Mumbai 400 049. India
Tel: +91 9022208074
eMail: info@zenpublications.com
Website: www.zenpublications.com

Prepared by: Ananda Wood
A-1 Ashoka, 3 Naylor Road,
Pune 411 001, India
eMail: woodananda@gmail.com

Ananda Wood is currently a moderator on the Advaitin e-group. Most of his books and articles may be accessed at http://sites.google.com/site/advaitaenquiry/

ISBN-13 978-81-88071-49-4

Contents

Preface

Do we know anything that is plainly and simply true, without any of the 'ifs' and 'buts' that complicate everything we perceive through our limited and uncertain personalities?

And is it thus possible to find any common basis of knowledge on which we can always rely, no matter what particular conditions and uncertainties surround our little bodies, senses and minds in a much larger universe?

The Upanishads are early texts that describe just such an enquiry into plain truth. However, there are two problems which complicate our understanding of these texts today.

First, they were composed at a time when knowledge was largely expressed in the imaginative metaphors of myth and ritual. Thus, along with their philosophical enquiry, the Upanishads also describe an archaic mythical and ritual context. It is from this archaic context that the enquiry was made, in times that are now long passed.

And second, as the founding texts of a very old philosophical tradition, they are expressed in a highly condensed way: which leaves them rather open to interpretation and explanation. The condensed statements of the Upanishads were called 'shruti' or 'heard'; because they were meant to be learned by hearing them directly from a living teacher, who would recite and interpret the words. Having received such a statement of condensed philosophical teaching, a student was meant to think about it over and over again, through a sustained process of individual reflection and enquiry. Eventually, after passing through many stages of thinking and rethinking the questions involved, the student was meant to come at last to a thorough and independent understanding of the statement, in his or her own right.

In the two and a half thousand years or more since the Upanishads began to be composed, their original statements have been interpreted and explained in many different ways, through many different schools of thought. Some schools have emphasized a religious approach to truth, through devotion to a worshipped God. Some schools have emphasized a mystical approach, through exercises of meditation that cultivate special states of experience beyond the ordinary limitations of our minds. And some schools emphasize a philosophical approach, through reasoned enquiry into common experience.

This book is focused on the philosophical approach. It follows Shrī Shankara's Advaita Vedānta tradition, as interpreted by Shrī Ātmānanda, a modern advaita philosopher who lived in Kerala State, India, 1883-1959.

The book is a collection of retellings from selected passages of the Upanishads. In these retellings, the rather compressed ideas of the original texts have been freely interpreted and elaborated, and often modified, to make them more accessible to a modern reader. Naturally, there is a price to be paid for such interpretation and modification. Since traditional ideas have thus been freely expressed in modern terms, the reader should understand that the retellings differ somewhat in their manner of expression from the traditional approach that is found in the originals.

For those who are interested in the original texts, a companion volume, called *Interpreting the Upanishads*, shows how particular concepts and passages have been interpreted in the retellings. For each passage discussed in the companion volume, a cross reference is given in a footnote at the beginning of the relevant retelling.

Hence this book and its companion volume form a pair, with cross-references between them. However, each volume can be read quite independently of the other.

Like the original texts, the book is perhaps best read as an anthology of collected passages. Because of their condensed expression, the Upanishads are meant to be thought about selectively, concentrating attention on one passage at a time. In various different passages, the same fundamental principles are approached again and again, in various different ways. Thus, one is free to pick out a particular passage that suits one's interests and one's state of mind at the time.

The trick is to avoid confusing the differing approaches through which the Upanishads ask different questions about one common truth. Then one can concentrate on those particular passages and those particular questions that hold one's attention sufficiently for the hard thinking that the subject requires.

From the Aitareya Upanishad

Self-questioning

Without me here, to know experience,
how could this experience be?

And how do I continue on?

If it's by speech that words are said,
if odours are perceived by smell …

if sights are seen by sense of vision,
sounds are heard by sense of hearing,
feelings felt by sense of touch,
and thoughts conceived by changing mind …

if thoughts and sense-perceptions are
absorbed within by understanding,
and appearances are formed
by mind's expressive thoughts and acts …

then who, or what, am I?

from 1.3.11

Realization

That which was born sees many things;
but what is here that's alien?

What does one really want to say?

By asking questions in this way,
the principle we each call 'I'
and absolute reality,
pervading all experience,
are realized as: 'This alone
that, truly, I have always known.'

from 1.3.13

Consciousness [1]

What is this self
to which we pay such heed?

Is it that which sees
or hears or senses
our perceptions
of the world?

Does it speak?
Does it tell taste *from*
from tastelessness? *3.1.1*

Or is it mind and heart:
which we describe as wisdom,
judgement, reason, knowledge,
learning, vision, constancy,
thought, consideration, motive,
memory, imagination, purpose,
life, desire, vitality?

These are but names *from*
for consciousness. *3.1.2*

Consciousness is everything:
God, all the gods,
the elements of which the world is made,
creatures and things of every kind,
however large or small,
however born or formed,
including all that breathes, walks, flies,
and all that moves or does not move.

All these are known by consciousness,
and take their stand in consciousness.

[1] See *Interpreting the Upanishads*, pages 6-10, for an indication of how this retelling interprets the original text.

Coming after consciousness,
the whole world stands in consciousness.

Consciousness is all there is. *from 3.1.3*

One who knows self,
as consciousness,
has risen from
this seeming world
to simple truth:

where all desires
are attained
and deathlessness
is realized. *from 3.1.4*

From the Kaṭha Upanishad

Death and 'the unconscious' [1]

Naciketas was a young Brahmin, blessed with a bright and cheerful temperament. But, on occasion, he was given to moods of intense thought. During one of these moods, when he was still a child, he had been asked what he was thinking about. He had some difficulty replying, but after a while he said:

'I don't quite know. That's what I keep trying to find out. But the harder I try, the less I seem to know. In the end, it seems that my mind knows nothing at all.'

It was this answer that earned him the name 'Naciketas', which means 'the unconscious'.

When Naciketas was on the verge of manhood, his father had become tired of material possessions and wished for better things. So a great sacrifice was held, to give all worldly wealth away.

As the family's cattle were being taken away, Naciketas felt greatly disturbed. He thought:

'These cattle need water to drink and fodder to eat. They need to be milked. And they aren't quite able to look after themselves. Surely it's we who should be looking after them, and the rest of our family inheritance. Will it really bring us happiness to give up our responsibilities like this? Perhaps father wants no further responsibility for me either.'

So Naciketas went up to his father and asked quietly: 'Father, to whom will you give me?'

Naciketas's father was busy with the well-wishers and admirers who surrounded him, and the question went unanswered. So Naciketas repeated it, a little louder. But now, as it became apparent that Naciketas was insisting on saying something out of place, an awkward silence followed. In this silence, Naciketas repeated his question a third time, with the most embarrassing clarity.

[1]See *Interpreting the Upanishads*, pages 156-157, 201-202 and 142-145, for an indication of how parts of this retelling interpret the original text (in particular: 2.1-2, 2.7-9 and 3.1,3-4, respectively).

In a fit of anger, his father replied: 'So, young man, your ego has got the better of you. There is only one thing to do with such an inflated ego. Go give it to death, where it belongs.'

At this, Naciketas turned round and walked away. He walked on for many hours, paying little attention to where he was going. Instead, he kept trying to make sense of his father's enraged pronouncement, and how to act in accordance with it:

'This little self that feels so young
now goes to death before its time,
ahead of those it knows and loves....

'But it is only one among
the many mortal things that are
inevitably going to die....

'What should poor mind and body do
when they are given up for dead?...

'By looking back into the past
and looking on as time proceeds,
we see that personality,
like corn, grows up from seed, gets ripe
and dies; producing further seed *from*
from which it is then born again....' *1.1-6*

By evening, Naciketas had walked far from home, into a range of forested hills without fields or villages or any other sign of human habitation, except for the forest path along which he walked. He came upon a cave and entered inside, to rest the tired body that was now beginning to obtrude into his thoughts. The cave was comfortable, and he noticed that someone had been there before him; for three stones had been arranged to form a fireplace, with some burnt-out cinders and ash left in between. But such details passed only briefly before his mind. His overwhelming preoccupation was with death, to which he had been given.

He spent three nights alone in the cave, venturing out into the forests during the day. He bathed and drank at the forest streams, but made no effort to find food, for he was kept from hunger by the mounting intensity of his thoughts.

As the third night gave way to morning, he awoke in a curiously calm and composed state of mind. In the preceding days, his contemplation of death had been erratic: one moment shrinking away in fear and regret, another moment coming back resolutely to the inevitable subject. Gradually, the thought of death grew more and more continuous, until there seemed to be nothing else but death. And then, finally, this all-embracing thought of death itself dissolved, into a state of consciousness where no perception, thought or feeling appeared at all....

When Naciketas came to, he felt a sense of radiant happiness that seemed to far outshine anything he had ever experienced before. But he soon noticed that there was someone else in the cave, looking at him with an inquisitive air of amused concern.

'It's all very well,' said the stranger, 'to go off on such a high-flying trip; but you look as though you could do with a bite to eat.'

Naciketas was in fact both hungry and thirsty by now; so he gratefully accepted the food and the bowl of water that he was offered. When he had finished eating, the stranger asked who he was and what had brought him here.

As Naciketas told his story, the stranger listened with great interest. Then, when the story was told, he asked: 'Well, what are you going to do now?'

'I'm not sure,' replied Naciketas. 'Perhaps you can give me some advice.'

'Perhaps I can. But first, it's best to be clear what you really want. Suppose you had three wishes. What would you choose? Take your time, and think carefully about it. After all, this cave is my home and you're a welcome guest. I've been away, and haven't been able to offer you any hospitality for the three nights you've been here, without any food. To make amends, I'll help you with your three wishes. So choose them well.'

After a short silence, Naciketas said: 'First, I wish my father peace of mind, and I wish that he should be reconciled with the son whom he has given to death.'

The stranger laughed: 'You shouldn't have much difficulty here. Your father must already have forgotten most of his anger; and it is only natural that he will feel relieved and pleased to have you back home again.'

Next, Naciketas described his second wish:

'In dreams and visions, it is said,
a heavenly state has been revealed:

'where age and death and thirst and hunger
don't arise; where happiness
becomes complete, unspoiled by any
trace of fear or misery.

'It's further said this stainless state
is reached by fire of sacrifice.

'Here, though I feel it true on faith,
I do not know quite what is meant.
Can you, who have renounced the world,
explain this sacrificial fire *from*
that leads from death to deathlessness?' *1.7-13*

'Alright,' said the stranger, 'I'll tell you what I know. There are three ways in which this fire can be understood. First, as you've heard, it is a means of attaining the infinite. Second, it is the universal fire on which all creation is founded. And third, it is the individual fire within each person's heart.'

He then explained to Naciketas the ritual of the fire sacrifice: showing how the various parts of the altar and the various actions of the ritual represent the elements and actions that make up the entire universe. In particular, he explained the fire on the altar as representing the creative energy that burns up the old and forms the new. After this, he paused a little and asked: 'Well, do you understand what I've been saying?'

'I think so,' replied Naciketas. 'You seem to be saying that the fire on the altar is a means for directing thought towards the infinite energy on which all creation is based.'

'Yes,' said the stranger, 'this infinite energy is at once the highest goal of thought and the underlying foundation of all created things. But then, what could it be within each person's heart?'

Naciketas thought a bit, and said: 'Perhaps it is the energy that makes a person sacrifice one thing for another, which is somehow implied to be of greater value.'

The stranger was visibly pleased: 'Yes, that's very well put. It's not for nothing that your name "Naciketas" means "the unconscious". For that is what this three-fold fire is. It is the fire of "the unconscious".

'Seen from outside, through body, sense
and mind, the heart seems dark within.
For objects are all seen outside,
and none appear within the heart.

'Thus, in the heart, there only seems
unconsciousness of outside things.

'And yet, this same "unconsciousness"
is all creation's blazing source:
of energy that forms the world,
and light that shows appearances.

'Now that you know this triple fire –
above, below and deep within –
you hold the chain of happenings
that make world's many-seeming forms.

'When all appearances are burned
in sacrificial fire within,
what must be done has then been done
and unity has been attained.

'Thus crossing over birth and death,
the unconditioned, stainless light
of all reality is known
and final peace is realized.

'Whoever knows this inner fire
throws off all seeming bonds of death
and lives, untouched by pain and grief, *from*
in unconditioned happiness.' *1.14-18*

Neither spoke for a while, as Naciketas tried to absorb what he had just heard. Then the stranger asked: 'Well, what about your third wish?'

Naciketas wanted to know more:

'When someone seems to pass away
beyond the world our senses see,
beyond the thoughts our minds conceive,
does that same person still exist?

'Just how can someone dead and gone
continue to exist at all?
What in a person could exist
when mind and body have passed on?

'How can experience carry on
where body does not speak or act,
where senses don't perceive a world,
where mind no longer thinks or feels …

'where differences, like birth and death
or pain and pleasure, don't arise …
where all appearances dissolve *from*
in what seems mere "unconsciousness"?' *1.19-20*

The stranger replied: 'Naciketas, think again. This is your last wish. Is this all that you want? Must you go on asking these subtle questions that have always been beyond the reach of all our physical and mental faculties? Why not ask for something else?'

'As you say,' said Naciketas, 'I am asking for knowledge that is beyond the reach of all physical and mental capability. What more could I ask? And if I don't ask you, whom else could I ask?'

'Perhaps,' said the stranger, 'you don't quite realize how far your capabilities extend. And so, perhaps you haven't fully considered the choices that you can make.

'In ordinary life, death is usually seen from a long way off, through an obscuring haze of fear and uncertainty. And then, of course, it seems that death is just a devouring beast, which only takes things away. But, seen from closer up, death turns out to be an overwhelmingly generous host. The more one overcomes one's fears and the better one gets to know death for what it is, the greater become one's powers and choices.

'You've come a long way on this road, Naciketas; and that gives you great powers of will and choice.

'You could put these powers to some constructive use: by gaining wealth and building a fine home; by having a family and bringing up children and grandchildren; by living a harmonious, prosperous life and influencing others to spread prosperity and harmony.

'And further, you could seek fulfilment by cultivating your sensibilities and purifying your character. Thus, you would attain glorious experiences of imagination and beauty, and you would rise to elevated states of goodness and clarity: far beyond the gross superficiality of ordinary, material satisfactions.

'There is so much in life from which to choose, by going out to meet the world and thus cultivating your interests and imagination. Why turn your back on all the good things of life? Why must you insist on asking questions about death?'

Naciketas was hardly able to contain himself:

'All these "good things" belong to death;
for each of them must change and pass.
There's death in every one of them.

'If I choose any one of them,
I'm choosing death, unknowingly.
I can't be satisfied with this.

'When mind and senses fade and die,
the world they see must disappear.
No wealth, nor family, nor any
cultivation then appears,
nor anything that world contains.

'All that we have is brought to us,
and taken back, by change and death.
It's death that gives and death that takes;
all seeming life is ruled by death.
All is achieved by knowing death.

'No object that the mind desires,
no pleasure that the mind enjoys,
no beauty that it seems to see,
can satisfy this restless mind.

'For mind is changing all the time;
its nature is its restlessness.
If mind is stilled, thought disappears;
and then there isn't any mind.

'Why make believe that mind lives on;
when every moment thought must die,
as it gives on to further thought
which in its turn must die again?

'As old things pass and new things rise,
what truly lives, through change and death,
that fresh, new life seems born again?

'I have no choice. I *have to* ask *from*
how death leads on to deathlessness.' *1.21-29*

'So,' said the stranger, 'you've made a distinction. On the one hand, body, senses and mind are attracted by a variety of changing purposes and enjoyments. On the other hand, as these changing attractions keep dying away, they express a continuing principle of value: which is the final, undying basis of all physical, sensual and mental desires.

'And what you want is to know this deathless basis of value, beneath the changing desires that it motivates.

'You've chosen well to seek this truth.
Not many hear it; and, of those,
not many rightly understand.

'For precious few are blessed to find
a teacher who can show this truth.

'And even when thus plainly shown,
only a few want truth enough
to overcome the fears that rise *from*
as ego's self-deceptions die. *2.1-7*

'Truth is approached in different ways;
and therefore it cannot be taught
by one who does not know it well,
beyond the ways that lead to it.

'It's subtler than the subtlest thing
that any faculty perceives;
and therefore it cannot be reached
without the help of someone else
who's gone beyond all faculties
of body or of sense or mind.

'It's known beyond all argument
when it is shown by someone else,
as nothing else but self alone:
which different people share alike
beneath all changing faculties *from*
of body and of sense and mind. *2.8-9*

'Found deep within each seeming thing,
it cannot be itself perceived
as any kind of seeming thing.

'For it is all reality:
the final, underlying base
of everything we seem to see.

'Beginningless, before all time,
it is the timeless principle
that stays the same through time and change, *from*
the background of each changing mind. *2.10-11*

'Here deep within each mind and heart,
it is the final, inner core
of unconditioned consciousness;
beneath all feelings and all thoughts
that motivate all living acts
and qualify what is perceived.

'It's known as knowing self alone,
whose very being is to shine,
self-evident, unlimited, *from*
unmixed with any alien thing. *2.12*

'When truth is heard and understood,
the nature of reality
is seen exactly as it is;
and dying personality
comes home in joy to deathless self,
the source of peace and happiness.

'As far as I can tell, this home *from*
is open to Naciketas.' *2.13*

Naciketas asked:

'Tell me this unconditioned truth:
beyond what's good or isn't good,
beyond what's done or isn't done,
beyond what causes or is caused, *from*
beyond all past or future time.' *2.14*

The stranger replied:

'The self within each mind and heart
is nothing else but consciousness.

'It is not born. It does not die.
It does not come from anything;
does not give on to anything.

'It simply *is*: before all time,
without beginning, change or end.
All thought of time depends on it;
but it does not depend on time,
and time does not apply to it.

'Though body's born, the self is not.
Though body acts, the self does not. *from*
Though body dies, the self does not. *2.18*

'So, if a killer thinks "I kill",
or if a victim thinks "I'm killed",
they neither of them think quite right. *from*

'Self does not kill, nor is it killed. *2.19*

'Far subtler than all subtlety,
much greater than all magnitude,
the self is here within each heart.

'It's known where knowledge is detached
from any kind of seeming act.

'Its nature shines as happiness,
when restless mind has come to peace
and, freed from grief and pain, dissolves *from*
in unconditioned consciousness. *2.20*

'Unmoved, self ranges far and wide,
throughout all space, throughout all time.

'It's here, in all experiences.
It's there, throughout the universe,
at every point of space and time.

'What else but unconditioned self
can know pure peace that does not change
or fade or die, but always shines;
thus motivating all that moves *from*
and lighting all that's ever seen? *2.21*

'Within each changing body, self
is bodiless, pure consciousness:

'the changeless, unconditioned base
from which all changing things are known,
the changeless, unconditioned base
on which all changing things appear.

'Whoever knows this simple truth
cannot be harmed by grief or pain. *from 2.22*

'This truth of self cannot be known
by scholarship or intellect
or any kind of discipline.
Since self is known by self alone,
it's found by merely choosing it.

'To one who truly wishes it,
the self reveals just what it is. *from 2.23*

'But egotism, ill intent,
disharmony, distracted mind
and restlessness are obstacles
that must somehow be overcome,
as self is sought and realized. *from 2.24*

'To one in search of final truth,
accomplishment and learning are
but nourishment, and death is but
a stimulus, towards the goal.

'Who knows where such a person is,
or where indeed this person goes? *from 2.25*

Ego and self

'Within each heart, there seem to be
two selves, experiencing the truth
of moral action in the world.

'Of these two selves, one is described
as a mere shadow or reflection
of the other self: the real
self, which shines by its own light,
by its own pure intensity.

'The shadow self is seeming ego,
acting in a world outside,
enjoying good and suffering ill.

'Behind appearances of ego,
real self is consciousness:
unmixed with personality, *from*
unconditioned by the world. *3.1*

Personality as a chariot

'If changing personality
is thought of as a chariot,
then self is living consciousness
which rides within the chariot.

'Seen from outside, the chariot takes
the knowing self from place to place;
and thus moves on, for sake of self,
expressing purpose and desire.

'But, as it knows itself within,
the self remains unmoved, unchanged;
while world and chariot move and change.

'As known from self, the world goes by
in changing scenes of passing show,
like scenes a chariot passes through.

'Just as a chariot is but part
of changing world in which it moves,
so too each personality
is but an object in the world.

'A moving chariot's wheels turn round,
its body suffers strain and shock.
So too, a person's body suffers
change and harm, and gets worn out.

'Just as a chariot's horses pull
it on to where it goes; so too
a person is pulled on by
sensual faculties and appetites,
towards the objects of desire.

'Just as a chariot's horses are
controlled by reins; so too, are
sensual faculties and appetites
controlled by the intent of will.

'And as the driver of a chariot
pulls upon the reins, to guide
the chariot for the traveller's sake;

'so too, the intellect and heart
think thoughts and feel emotions that
direct the will, all for the sake
of knowing self that lives within.

'The chariot's body, horses, reins
and driver are all changing objects
acting in an outside world,
of which they are but little parts.

'So too, a person's body, senses,
will and intellect and heart
are changing objects, each of which
acts as a partial piece of world.

'The self within is consciousness.
Known truly, as it knows itself,
it does not move; it does not change.
It is no part of changing world.
It only knows; it does not act.

'Its knowledge is no kind of act;
its very being is to shine.
It shines itself, by its own light;
and it is nothing else but light.

'It's this pure light of consciousness
that lights up all appearances,
as body, sense and mind seem to
perceive a world of seeming things.

'By false identity of self
as changing body, sense and mind,
the consciousness of knowing self
seems mixed with body's sensual acts
and with the acts of thought and feeling
carried out by changing mind.

'And thus, confusing changeless self
with changing personality,
experience seems conditioned by
a physical and mental world
of forms and names and qualities
that bodies sense and minds conceive.

'Through such conditioned consciousness
a person seems to taste the fruit
of good and bad experiences:
enjoying what seems to be good *from*
and suffering that which seems ill. *3.3-4*

Condit-ioning and consc-iousness

'But can conditioned consciousness
be truly consciousness at all?

'What seems conditioned consciousness
is not the light of knowing self,
but just the seeming, passing acts
of body, sense and mind in world.

'Each seeming act is lit by self:
whose nature is pure consciousness,
unmixed with body, sense or mind.

'This consciousness is always here,
in all of our experience.
It lights each seeming thing we see.

'It is the knowing base that always
carries on; as changing objects
are perceived, and changing feelings,
thoughts, perceptions come and go.

'It is the stable base on which
all variations are compared
and different things are told apart.

'Beneath all change and difference
of objects that appear perceived
by body, sense and mind, it is
the background of experience:

'where all appearances must rise,
on which each one of them depends,
and where they all are taken in.

'Upon this base of consciousness,
all qualities and names and forms
appear, conditioning the world
perceived by heart and mind and sense.

'It underlies conditioning.
Conditions can't arise at all
unless they're lit by consciousness;

'unless they are related and
compared, upon the common basis
of continuing consciousness.

'Conditions don't apply to it,
nor qualities or names or forms,
nor any change or difference.

'All these arise from consciousness.

'Like all appearances, they must
depend on consciousness to be
perceived; and then, as they are
understood, they're taken in, dissolved
in consciousness from which they come.

'Upon this base of consciousness
all different-seeming things appear.

'It is the common basis where
such different-seeming things relate,
as parts or part appearances
of more complete reality.

'It is the common principle
that's there in all experience,
beneath all mere appearances
of different things in seeming world.

'It is complete reality:
where all apparent things relate
in underlying unity,
beneath all mere appearances
perceived by body, sense and mind.

'On consciousness, all things are based.
In consciousness, all things are found.
Beneath what seems, all that is known
is unconditioned consciousness.

'Within each personality,
all different-seeming faculties
of sense and mind depend on this
shared principle of consciousness.

'In all our various feelings, thoughts,
perceptions, purposes and acts,
it's consciousness that is expressed.

'It is the common, stable base
on which our feelings, thoughts, perceptions,
purposes and actions are
co-ordinated and controlled.
On it depend all meaningful
coherence and integrity.

'Wherever common consciousness
is found expressed in different parts
of personality, these parts
are thereby integrated in
one living, individual whole.

'Thus it is consciousness that
unifies each individual life.
It is the essence of each
person's individuality.

'And yet, it is impersonal
within each personality.

'Because it is the base on which
all personality appears,
it cannot be at all confined
in any personality.

'Because it is the knowing base
of all experiences of time
and space and change and difference,
it cannot be confined by time
or space or change or difference.

'Since quality and name and form
do not condition it at all,
there's nothing to distinguish it
in different personalities:
whose only differences are those
of form and name and quality.

'It is the same in all of us:
impersonal, the common base
on which we all rely, to put
together and communicate *from*
our various different points of view. *3.5-9*

Levels of identity

'If body is identified
as knowing self, it seems that
consciousness consists in body's
outward acts toward material things.
And thus, an outward world seems known.

'But body is itself an object.
It is just an instrument
through which the senses see the world.

'If senses are identified
as knowing self, it seems that
consciousness consists in sense-perceptions
of a world that's shown by sights
and sounds and smell and taste and touch.

‘But senses are themselves just objects.
They are only instruments
that bring sensations to the mind.
Thus mind perceives a world outside,
interpreting what senses show.

‘If mind is next identified
as knowing self, it seems that
consciousness consists in the perceptions,
thoughts and feelings that appear
and disappear within our minds.

‘And here, it seems, a world is known
where meaning, thought and feeling are
expressed by life in outward things.

‘But even mind is just an object.
It is just an instrument
by which appearances are formed
in our experience of the world.

‘In everyone’s experience,
only a part or aspect of
the world appears at any time.

‘As time proceeds, the world seems known
through a progressive stream of part
appearances, formed by the mind
as it perceives and thinks and feels.

‘At any given point of time,
when only part of world appears,
how can the rest of world be known
and somehow taken into count?

‘That which appears seems known by mind.
But knowledge which does not appear
is taken to be understood,
beneath the surface of attention,
at the background of experience
underlying seeming mind.

'Such background understanding seems
to comprehend far more than what
appears to mind at any time;

'and thus it seems a store of knowledge
which can grow with time, so that
we get to know more of the world.

'If understanding is identified
as knowing self, it seems
that consciousness consists of knowledge
which can be developed and
increased: to know more of
reality, beneath appearances.

'But understanding too is just
an object. It is just an
instrument, assimilating different
views and thus developing
expanded, deeper views that seem *from*
to show more of reality. *3.10*

'As different views are understood,
they each become absorbed into
the background of experience,
beneath the surface of the mind.

'And from this background, understanding
is expressed in feelings, thoughts
and acts that lead to further views;
which in their turn are taken in
and add to what we understand.

'What is this background, into which
perceptions are absorbed, and from
which understanding is expressed?

'Here, at the background of the mind,
appearances are not perceived.
No object can appear at all.

'This background is unmanifest.
And thus at first it seems there's
nothing here, except unconsciousness.

'But more exactly seen, what we
have here, beneath the mind, is just
unconsciousness of objects that
appear perceived by changing mind.

'Here, at the background of the mind,
apparent objects aren't perceived;
but what we know continues on,
while seeming objects come and go.

'Here, at the background of the mind,
where what we know is understood,
there must of course be consciousness;

'but it is not perception, thought
or feeling of the seeming things
that come into appearance at
the changing surface of our minds.

'Instead, it's consciousness unmixed
with any seeming object that
appears and disappears in mind.

'It is just consciousness, which knows
only itself, just as it really is:
beneath all mere appearances *from*
that come and go before our minds. *3.11*

Non-duality

'Viewed at the surface of our minds,
it seems that consciousness is mixed
with changing objects that it knows.

'But as it knows itself within,
unchanged by mere appearances,
it always is pure consciousness:
unmixed with any other thing.

'All feelings, thoughts, perceptions are
appearances of consciousness.

'All these appearances reflect
its self-illuminating light,
as they appear to show a world
of many different-seeming things.

'But no appearance can exist
apart from knowing consciousness.
Any appearance that departs
from it immediately dissolves
and is no longer there at all.

'Thus no appearance has any
existence outside consciousness.
It is the sole reality
that each appearance truly shows.

'All the appearances we see
are nothing else but consciousness.
And all the world they seem to show
is nothing else but consciousness.

'It is complete reality
that's shown by all appearances.

'As it illuminates appearances
and thus appears to light
the world, it only knows itself, *from*
unmixed with any alien thing. *3.12*

'Where self is known as consciousness,
all of reality is known
as nothing else but knowing self.

'Here, self is one with all that's known,
and unconditioned happiness *from*
of deathless truth is realized.' *3.15*

Self-discovery [2]

It seems our senses are created
looking out: from self within
towards a world that's known outside.

And so, it seems we only see
external objects in the world,
as they appear to outward sense.

At first, it seems there is no way
to see the self that knows within,
the self from which all seeing comes.

But one brave person, seeking
deathlessness, turned sight back in, towards
the inner source from which sight comes;

and thus the self was truly seen:
as unconditioned consciousness, *from*
from which all seeming things arise. *4.1*

[2]See *Interpreting the Upanishads*, pages 122-123, for an indication of how this retelling interprets the original text.

Desire and enquiry [3]

Outward desires lead the mind
into the widespread snare of death:
which rules this world of seeming things
that come to be and pass away.

But those of steadfast courage do
not rest content with the pretence
of relative stability,
sought here among unstable things.

Instead, they question all pretence
until true certainty is found:
beyond the reach of change and death, *from*
beyond all trace of fear and doubt. *4.2*

Perception

The self is that same principle
of consciousness by which are known
all forms, all tastes, all smells, all sounds,
all feelings, pleasures we perceive;
when we're awake or when we dream.

With self thus known unlimited
in everything, here at the centre
of all life, throughout all time;

how then can fear or grief arise? *from 4.3-5*

[3]See *Interpreting the Upanishads*, page 157, for an indication of how this retelling interprets the original text.

Difference

What's true in here is true out there.
What's there, in truth, is also here.
Truth is the same, both here and there.

Wherever differences are seen,
perceiving ego suffers change *from*
and thus goes on from death to death. *4.10*

But when mind turns back to its source,
it knows itself as consciousness,
unmixed with any other thing.

And then it is quite evident
that, though appearances differ,
reality remains the same. *from*

No difference is really there. *4.11*

Dissipation and purity

As water rained upon a height
flows down the mountain-sides, dispersed;

so too the ego dissipates, *from*
perceiving different-seeming things. *4.14*

As water poured into itself
retains its natural purity;

so also thought reflecting back
to consciousness, from which it comes,
retains the purity of self *from*
which is at one with what it knows. *4.15*

The living self

Within this personality,
of seeming body, sense and mind,
is consciousness that was not born
and can't be twisted or deformed.

It is just that which does not grieve, *from*
was always free, and is free now. *5.1*

It is just that which shines in light;
which carries on through space and time;
which is the goal of sacrifice;

which must be honoured in a guest;
which makes a home; which lives in men
and gods, in heaven's justice, and
in nature's ordered harmony.

It's all that matters or is true
in anything that has been born:

whether arisen from the earth,
or formed in waters' changing flow,
or manifesting nature's laws, *from*
or fallen from some higher state. *5.2*

All living action, outward-going
or reflecting back within,
must finally begin and end
with unconditioned consciousness:

which is expressed in every act
and is the cause of every change,
but never acts and stays unchanged *from*
here at the heart of everything. *5.3*

When body dies and body's acts
no longer seem to see a world,
nor tell the world what they have seen,

what then remains of that which lived
and was expressed in body's acts?

That which remains is consciousness:
the unconditioned, inner self, *from*
unmixed with world's appearances. *5.4*

No dying thing can live through actions,
outward bound or turned back in.

In outward and reflected acts,
all life expresses consciousness:

from which all living actions rise,
on which their meaning must depend, *from*
in which they end and come to rest. *5.5*

The principle of individuality[4]

What is the individual
life principle that carries on
behind the changing mask of
seeming personality? It is
just this: which always is awake,
while other things dissolve in sleep.

From it arises each desire
that seeks some narrow, passing goal,
and thus clouds personality
with incompleteness seeking change.

But in itself it's always clear;
for it is all reality:
which stays the same, undimmed, unchanged,
beneath all mere appearances.

It's that alone which does not die.

In it, all seeming worlds are based. *from*
Apart from it, there's nothing else. *5.8*

Just as one common principle
of underlying energy
is there throughout the universe,
appearing in the different forms
that are so differently perceived
in different objects and events;

so too, one common principle
of underlying consciousness
is here throughout experience,
appearing in the different forms
that are so differently perceived
in different personalities.

[4]See *Interpreting the Upanishads*, pages 106-110, for an indication of how this retelling interprets the original text.

This underlying consciousness,
which different people share alike
beneath all their conditionings,
is every person's real self.

It's here in body, sense and mind
and yet it is beyond them all. *from 5.9-10*

Just as the sun lights what we see,
quite unaffected by the failings
of a person's sense of sight;

so too, the self lights all experience,
unaffected by the failings
of perception, thought and feeling
in our senses and out minds. *from 5.11*

In course of time, as different actions,
thoughts and feelings come and go,
they are co-ordinated by
this underlying consciousness
of self, which is their common base
beneath their seeming differences.

This is the common basis where
all different persons, and the
various objects that they see, relate.

It is from here that different things
and different persons are seen
functioning together, in an
ordered and intelligible world.

And it is only this, one self
of underlying consciousness,
whose essence is made manifest
in all the many forms of world.

By turning inwards, this one truth
is seen, already standing here:
as one's own self. Just this, and
only this, brings lasting happiness. *from 5.12*

It is the continuity
that is implied by changing things;

the changeless base of consciousness
implied by changing mental states;

the changeless, partless unity
which all diversity implies,
and which alone fulfils desire.

By turning inwards, this one truth
is seen, already standing here:
as one's own self. Just this, and *from*
nothing else but this, brings lasting peace. *5.13*

It is conceived as 'that out there':
as all the world's reality
beneath all mere appearances.

And it's conceived as 'this in here':
as ever-present consciousness,
by which appearances are known.

But both of these, 'this' consciousness
and 'that' reality, are always
present here together: at all times,
in everyone's experience.

Thus being always here together,
they can never be distinguished.
Though we call them by two names,
they are not two, but only one.

This final non-duality,
of knowing self and all that's known,
is unconditioned happiness;
for here completeness has been found.

How then can it be truly known,
as it shines out from self within *from*
and is reflected back from world? *5.14*

It does not shine by light of sun
or moon or stars or burning fire.
It shines alone, by its own light.

Without it, nothing else can shine;
for it lights all appearances:
which shine as its reflected light.

Thus all the world is nothing else
but the reflected light of self.

As self illuminates the world,
it just illuminates itself.

Through all the world's appearances,
this self-illuminating light
remains always unchanged, unmixed *from*
with anything beside itself. *5.15*

Living energy [5]

The whole created universe
is made of living energy
that moves and oscillates and shines.

This boundless store of restless
cosmic energy has terrible
destructive power. It's like an
upraised thunderbolt: to petty
ego's fragile life, identified
with little body, sense and mind.

But if, transcending petty ego,
all the world is known as life –
as only living energy –
then how can death arise at all?

For one who knows the world like this,
as only life, there is no death.

In truth, there's only deathlessness. *from 6.2*

[5]See *Interpreting the Upanishads*, pages 82-83, for an indication of how this retelling interprets the original text.

Self-purification

The senses that perceive the world
are changing objects in the world.

They are objective instruments
through which the world is known by self.

As objects acting in the world,
they are a part of changing world. *from*
They are not part of knowing self. *6.6*

Beyond the senses is the mind,
to which the senses seem to bring
sensations from an outside world.

But mind, too, is an instrument
that acts within the changing world,
interpreting what senses see.

As something acting in the world,
mind is a part of changing world.
It is not part of knowing self.

Beyond the mind is character
which also acts within the world,
to motivate both mind and sense
towards the objects they perceive.

Thus character, like mind and sense,
is an objective instrument
through which the changing world is known.
It is not part of knowing self.

Beyond all varied character
is universal principle,
which different characters must share
to make their differences relate.

Such common principle as well,
may be perceived as part of world:
as an objective instrument
that acts to put together world
from different appearances.

Perceived like this, as part of world,
it is not part of knowing self.

Beyond such common principle,
we think of the 'unmanifest':
as that which carries on unthought
beneath the surface of the mind,
through changing thought of seeming world.

But even this 'unmanifest'
may be conceived as part of world,
as an objective instrument:

which acts unseen, here at the background
of all change, as the support
that must continue on through change,
to show the changes that take place.

And thus conceived, as part of world, *from*
it is not part of knowing self. *6.7*

Beyond this too, which is thus called
'unmanifest', is knowing self:
whose nature is pure consciousness,
unmixed with any part of world.

It is here in all experience,
always present everywhere:

quite unconditioned and unchanged
by changing world's appearances *from*
of name and form and quality. *6.8*

'Unmanifest' to outward-going
mind and sense; it's known through thought
that turns back in, and is dissolved
in unconditioned consciousness:

which simply manifests itself
as self and all reality.

They who know this find that they're free,
as they have always truly been, *from*
beyond all thought of death and grief. *6.9*

Meditation

When mind and senses cease to act,
no seeming object can appear.

Then, consciousness shines out alone,
unmixed with those appearances
that make it seem what it is not.

This state of unmixed consciousness
is said to be the highest state;

and meditation is the art
of holding mind and senses back
to reach this state by act of will.

Thus, turning will towards a state
where all distractions are dissolved,
attention turns to consciousness:
which shines in all appearances,
and shines alone when they dissolve.

But when this state has passed away,
appearances return again;

and consciousness then seems obscured
just as it seemed to be before.

How can pure consciousness be known
for what it is, unmoved, unchanged:

no matter what distractions rise;
no matter what is seen or heard,
smelled, tasted, touched or thought or felt;
no matter what seems to appear *from*
to changing body, mind and sense? *6.10-11*

Understanding truth [6]

Mere talking cannot find out truth,
nor can ideas conceived by mind,
nor mere sensations of the world
impressed on mind by any sense.

If not by finding out from one
who knows it well, beyond all doubt,
and shows exactly what it is, *from*
how else can truth be understood? *6.12*

Truth is approached by telling what
is really there from what is not,
beneath what merely seems to be.

When truth has thus been told apart
from falsity, it's understood
as all that's real everywhere *from*
in everything that seems to be. *6.13*

When all desires are released
from ego's false identity
of self that is and mind that wants,

then truth shines here, within the heart, *from*
where all reality is found. *6.14*

Thus all the knots of heart are loosed;
and that which seemed to die turns out
to be, and to have always been, *from*
undying, unconditioned truth. *6.15*

[6]See *Interpreting the Upanishads*, page 200, for an indication of how part of this retelling interprets the original text (in particular 6.12).

The 'I'-principle [7]

The real self, the inmost
principle of personality,
is always present here at heart
in everyone's experience.

Each petty ego lives in fear
for its own false security
that clings to passing attributes
of changing personality.

But, putting ego's fears aside
with steadfast courage, one may choose
from one's own personality
that inner, unconditioned core
which does not fear or change or die *from*
and is one's true security. *6.17*

[7]See *Interpreting the Upanishads*, pages 118-119, for an indication of how this retelling interprets the original text.

From the Brihadāraṇyaka Upanishad

Non-duality [1]

That world out there, this self in here,
each is reality, complete:

from which arises everything,
to which all things return again,
in which all seeming things consist;

which stays the same, unchanged, complete.

from the peace invocation

[1]See *Interpreting the Upanishads*, pages 1-5, for an indication of how this retelling interprets the original text.

Prayer for truth

As priests recite the chanted word,
its meaning comes from prayer within:

'From untruth, lead me on to truth.
From darkness, bring me into light.
From death, take me to deathlessness.'

Death is merely non-existence;
truth is that which always is.
Death is but a dream of darkness
known by light that never dies.
In all our prayers for truth and light,
we seek no less than deathlessness.

Through many prayers and hymns of praise,
a worshipper seeks sustenance
and asks that wishes be fulfilled.

But, just to pray and understand,
this in itself fulfils desire
and finds unchanging deathlessness.

No want of world's success can raise *from*
false hopes, for one who prays and knows. *1.3.28*

Self and the absolute [2]

Right from the start, each person's self
is common, plain humanity:
which different-seeming persons share
through changing times and changing minds
in different personalities.

Whatever sights a person sees,
whatever may appear to mind,
in all of our experiences,
the self is always present there.

Thus nothing ever is perceived
without the presence of the self.
And nothing anyone perceives
can ever be apart from self.

First and foremost, every person
starts by thinking: 'This is I.'
And so each person is called 'I'.

When asked for one's identity,
what first response comes up at once,
spontaneously, from deep within?

One first identifies oneself as 'I',
and only then come other names
by which one is identified.

This, which comes first, before all things,
burns up all misery and wrong.
Anything that tries to push
in front of plain humanity *from*
burns up, for one who knows just this. *1.4.1*

But people seem to have known fear:
a lonely person feels afraid.

[2]See *Interpreting the Upanishads*, pages 36-48, for an indication of how this retelling interprets the original text.

When such a person, all alone,
observes 'Of what am I afraid,
if there is nothing else but I?';
then with this thought fear vanishes.

Without a second thing to fear, *from*
what is there to be frightened of? *1.4.2*

And people also seem to feel
unhappiness: a lonely person
suffers want of warmth and joy.

By longing for companionship,
life in this world has taken shape
as male and female intertwined.

The self has thus been made to seem
divided, fallen into two,
as male and female have been formed:
each one an uncompleted half.

Each one then suffers emptiness,
which must be filled by someone else.
So male and female join in one, *from*
and from this match we all are born. *1.4.3*

The knowing self in each of us
is underlying consciousness
from which appearances arise
in everyone's experience.

Since everything comes out of it,
it's that which seems to have become
this many seeming universe.
It's all creation in itself.

To know it is to stand as self,
which one has truly always been, *from*
at all creation's timeless source. *1.4.5*

The world we see is only this:
which is itself unmanifest.

Only by name and form has this
seemed to be manifest, as world.

The world seems manifested when
some seeming name is used for this,
some seeming form is seen in this.

This is that common principle
which permeates the universe
into each corner of the world;

just as a blade fits in its sheath,
or as the energy which forms
the universe lies there within
all matter that is formed by it.

This universal principle
cannot be known through force or power
of life's intentions, nor through speech,
nor sight, nor hearing, nor through mind.

These are merely names of functions:
each of which is incomplete.
Looking through such partial functions,
all that's seen is incomplete.

Such means can never quite know truth.

Reflecting on the self alone,
all partial functions merge in one.
In all the world that we perceive,
this self is what we need to reach:
for everything is known by this.

True honour, glory, grace, success
arise unasked for one who knows *from*
all things as signs of only this. *1.4.7*

Beyond all else, it is the self
that's near and dear: more than all wealth,
more than all friends and family.

When anything besides this self
is thought an object of desire,
then desire turns to torment:
even desire for God himself.

In any object of desire,
self is all we wish to find.

Where self is truly seen in love,
there love is found to be complete, *from*
for what is loved can never end. *1.4.8*

By knowledge of the absolute,
a person hopes to be complete.

This absolute we thus invoke,
what does it know, as it creates *from*
from its own self the world we see? *1.4.9*

The absolute is only this,
which first and foremost knows itself.

It knows: '*I am the absolute.*'

And on this base appear from it
the many things we seem to see.

Whoever realizes this,
and knows 'I am the absolute',
becomes complete in everything.

The gods themselves cannot undo
one who has found identity
with that which is their very self.

But if one heeds an alien god
who seems apart from one's own self,
truth can't be known; for then one is
a beast of burden to the gods.

As beasts of burden have their masters,
so do people have their gods.

It is not liked when any beast
is taken from its master's fold.
Nor is it liked when someone finds
this truth: that in each one of us *from*
the self is absolute, and free. *1.4.10*

It is this absolute that seems
to have evolved, through course of time,
as knowledge, power, enterprise
and service, in society.

We dream of gods to seek out worlds
of sublimated energy;
and in our waking life we seek
out knowledge of our universe.

For energy and learning are
both forms in which the absolute
has been expressed in what we see.

Blindness to our own existence
robs our lives of all reward;
every one of our achievements
must in time dissolve away.

But, if one only sees the self
absolute in all existence,
life's reward can never die.

Everything that is desired *from*
is produced from this same self. *1.4.15*

The world of beings is this self.

It is the mythic world of gods
created by religious rite.

It is the fancied world of thought
created by an author's words.

It is the world tradition makes
respecting past experience
and also seeking something new.

It is the world we humans make
from need for home and sustenance.

It is the world of animals,
where grass and water must be found.

It is the earth on which subsist
beasts, birds and other forms of life,
in bodies that are homes of this.

One should wish well of one's own world.
At heart, all beings do wish well,
seen in that light which knows just this.

Whatever anyone has known,
whatever anyone has sought *from*
to know, is nothing else but this. *1.4.16*

In truth, there is one single self,
with nothing else at all besides.

And yet, it seems that people seek
out company of other selves,
that people feel desire for birth
and property and gainful work.

Such limited desires can't
grow to be more than limited,
not even if one wants them to.

A lonely person wants to find
companionship, wants a new life,
wants things and looks for work to do.

And where such wishes aren't fulfilled,
a person does not feel complete.

How can a person be complete?

Through consciousness that's known as self;
through speech that's married to the self;
through purpose as its progeny.

Through property that, known by sight,
is known as nothing else but sight;
through worth that, known by sense, is known
as only sensibility.

Through work that shows true purity
of self, on which all life depends.

In all the multiplicity
of actions, persons, creatures, things,
throughout this many-seeming world,
the self is one and one alone.

All is reached, by knowing this. *from 1.4.17*

The source of experience

No matter how much of experience
is consumed by anyone,
it always seems there's something more:
some new experience to be had,
for those who are not satisfied.

But how is life thus infinite?
As previous life gets tired and dies,
what is the ever-living source
from which new life is seen to rise?

This source is the 'I'-principle:
the principle of knowing self,
within each personality.

It is the self that each calls 'I':
the inner, knowing principle
of unconditioned consciousness,
unmixed with any alien thing.

It's here in all experiences.
It must be here before perceptions,
thoughts or feelings can arise.
It carries on while these perceptions,
thoughts and feelings come and go.
And it remains, self-manifest,
when all of them have disappeared.

It's from this changeless principle
that all experiences arise.
On this they stand and seem to change.
And back to this they must return,
as they're consumed and taken in.

It is thus inexhaustible,
as it gives rise, time after time,
to all that's thought, perceived or felt.

As every person knows experience
in the course of passing time,
successive thoughts, perceptions, feelings
come to end and disappear,
each one succeeded by the next.

But consciousness is always here:
as that which knows, no matter what
seems to appear or disappear.

As feelings, thoughts, perceptions change,
pure consciousness continues on:
beneath all mere appearances
perceived through body, sense and mind.

And here, beneath appearances,
it knows things as they really are.

It does not know external things
through intervening faculties
of partial body, sense and mind,
which are believed to tell a tale
of some imagined world outside.

It knows directly, face to face;
for all it knows is known as self
that shines unmixed, by its own light.

from 1.5.2 – passage towards end

Mind, speech and life

Each person's self is manifested
in three ways: mind, speech and life.

Mind is the faculty that takes
attention out from consciousness
to partial objects in the world.

Without the mind's attention turned
to some apparent part of world,
no object could appear perceived,
nor thought about, nor felt at all.

Thus, even though light from an object
falls upon one's open eyes
and sharply focused images
are formed upon one's retinas,
that object still cannot appear
without attention from the mind.

If mind's attention is elsewhere
and does not turn to what eyes see,
then what is seen does not appear.

So too, if mind's attention does
not turn to what is heard by ear,
then what is heard does not appear.

Hence mind is that which makes appear
those parts of world to which it turns.

And it does this not only through
the body's sensual faculties
that see and hear, smell, taste and touch,
but also through its own internal
faculties that think and feel.

The mind directs attention by:
the things it chooses to desire,
how it conceives what's been perceived,
its doubts and pointed questioning,
what it believes and disbelieves,
where it holds fast and where lets go,
its sense of shame for its own wrongs,
its contemplation of the truth,
the fear that makes it want to run.

All these are aspects of the mind:
which first goes out to seeming world,
discriminating differences;

but then reflects attention back
in order to discern the truth
that touches mind from deep within.

Speech is the faculty expressing
meaning in our words and acts:
thus rising up from consciousness
to actions in the world outside.

All that is said and done, and all
that happens in the world, can be
correctly understood as speech.

For everything is understood
by asking what it really means;

by asking what it says to us:
as we reflect back to the
underlying source of consciousness,
from which all meaning rises up
in everyone's experience.

Thus, through conditioned words and acts
of seeming body, sense and mind,
the meaning that's conveyed expresses
unconditioned consciousness.

Life is the faculty of
living on through passing time, as old
experiences give rise to new.
It's life that lives, while time proceeds
and dying things all pass away.

As life goes on, its living acts
express undying consciousness,
out in the world of change and death.

Then, as the world reacts on life,
specific objects are perceived:
discarding waste from what is used
and thus creating partial views,
restricted needs and narrowed aims.

When different views have been perceived,
they are contrasted and compared:
disseminating information
and discerning what it means.

Discerning what has been perceived,
new meanings rise from consciousness:
expressed in new experiences,
as life aspires to better things.

As new experiences arise,
what has been learned is understood:
thus integrating past and future
and all different faculties
at the background of the mind,
where consciousness continues on
beneath all seeming change and death.

When someone says 'I think', 'I feel',
then self appears in seeming mind.
When someone says 'I say', 'I mean',
then self appears in speech and act.
When someone says 'I'm still alive',
then self appears in lasting life.

What is the common principle
of self that is thus manifest
in all these three: mind, speech and life?

This common principle of self
is unconditioned consciousness:

which lights all that appears through mind,
which underlies all words and acts, *from*
which lives unchanged through change and death. *1.5.3*

Speech, as what's said and done in world,
makes up this world that's known through mind.
Mind is the movement back and forth
between the world and consciousness.
But life is not quite in the world,
for it lives on in consciousness *from*
beyond the reach of changing mind. *1.5.4*

Speech, as expression in the world,
is just what's known through changing mind.
And mind, in turn, is that which one
should seek to know: reflecting back
to consciousness, from which mind comes.

But life cannot be known through mind;
for mind depends on living on,
to make the seeming world appear.

Thus life appears as the unknown, *from*
beneath the surface of the mind. *1.5.8-10*

The various different faculties
of changing personality
are but the property of self:
which lives within, unknown by mind.

It's only through these faculties
that self appears to move or change,
to grow, develop or decline.

In truth, the self is motionless
and does not change or act at all.
It's only faculties that act,
move, change, develop or decline.
The self is where they all are joined.

It is as if a wheel turns round
a centre: which remains unmoved,
but which supports the wheel and rim
from where the spokes all join in one.

So too the self, here at the centre
of all life, does not engage
in any kind of changing act;
while it supports the faculties
that join in it and radiate
into a world of changing acts.

Just as the spokes and rim revolve
about the centre of a wheel,
so too all faculties and world
revolve about the changeless self
where all things join and find support.

Thus, all that can in truth be lost
is only outward property.
Whatever property is lost
does not affect the living self, *from*
where all of life is to be found. *1.5.15*

As different faculties compete
for the attention of the mind,
they cannot all appear at once.
Instead, they rise successively.

Each one appears just for a while,
becomes exhausted and subsides;
so other faculties can rise.

Speech does not go on speaking all
the time; but speaks just for a while,
before it tires and dies away.
So too with sight and hearing and
with various other faculties.

These intermittent faculties
are all caught up in change and death.

They do not last; and to connect
they must depend on something else
that carries on through passing time
between their intermittent acts.

What is this continuity
of life: that carries on, between
our different, intermittent acts?

All faculties are only forms
of this one living principle
which does not change or die away.

Whatever moves or doesn't move,
whatever change seems to take place,
it is quite inexhaustible.

It does not suffer loss or harm.
It's not disturbed in any way.

No faculty compares with it.
Whoever goes against it gets *from*
cut off from life, dries up and dies. *1.5.21*

This changeless, living principle
is not, in truth, a faculty
that carries out some kind of act.

Instead, it is the knowing base,
of unconditioned consciousness:
from which all mind and faculties
arise, and into which they set.

It is, as it has always been,
the base of all reality,
the underlying truth of life:
which all that happens must express.

To realize it needs complete
resolve; to understand, throughout
all that is done and seen and thought
and felt, just what it means to say:

'I am this self which does not die.' *from 1.5.23*

Names, forms and acts

Three aspects of experience are:
first, *names* identifying things;
next, *forms* through which these names appear;
and third, the *acts* by which each thing
is seen to act on other things.

All names arise from saying things.
Speech is the underlying source
that's common to all different names.
It is their base, their ground support.

All forms arise from seeing things.
Sight is the underlying source
that's common to all different forms.
It is their base, their ground support.

All acts arise from what self is.
Self is the underlying source
that's common to all different acts.
It is their base, their ground support.

All three together are this self.
It's one in three, and three in one.
It is the deathless principle
that's here in all experience.

Found here within all name and form,
this principle is life itself, *from*
beyond the reach of seeming death. *1.6.1-3*

Cosmic faith and truth [3]

Bālāki Gārgya was a learned scholar. One day, he came to Ajātashatru, King of Kāshi, and said: 'I propose to speak with you about the absolute.'

Ajātashatru replied: 'For this, I grant you a thousand cattle.'

Gārgya began: 'I worship as the absolute that spirit which is seen in the sun.'

'Perhaps this is a little misleading,' replied Ajātashatru. 'It seems to me that the sun is worshipped as a radiant god who lives in the sky, shining light and warmth upon living creatures. Surely, such worship serves only to awaken interest in the pursuit of excellence, thus encouraging people to start raising themselves from the apathy and ignorance of unquestioning habit.'

Gārgya went on: 'I worship as the absolute that spirit which is seen in the moon.'

'Perhaps this is misleading again,' replied Ajātashatru. 'It seems to me that the moon is worshipped as a mysterious, white-robed god of other-worldly experience. Surely, such worship serves only to provide a profusion of subtle experiences, of which there is no end.'

Gārgya persisted: 'I worship as the absolute that spirit which is seen in lightning.'

'It seems to me,' replied Ajātashatru, 'that lightning is worshipped for its brilliance of concentrated energy. Surely, such worship amounts to nothing more than cultivating qualities of brilliance and power, and passing these qualities on to succeeding generations.'

'I worship as the absolute that spirit which is seen in the unbounded space of sky.'

'It seems to me that the sky is worshipped for its all-transcending elevation and for the fixed regularity of its stars. Surely, such worship amounts to nothing more than looking for regular patterns and laws of nature, which somehow transcend and thus govern the variations and changes of the apparent world.'

'I worship as the absolute that spirit which is seen in the invisible power of blowing wind.'

'It seems to me that the wind is worshipped for its irresistibility as it blows round objects. Surely, such worship amounts to nothing more than cultivat-

[3]See *Interpreting the Upanishads*, pages 26-27, for an indication of how the end of this retelling interprets the original text (2.1.20).

ing a sensitive and flexible attitude, of feeling one's way past obstacles that seem to come in the way of progress.'

'I worship as the absolute that spirit which is seen in burning fire.'

'It seems to me that fire is worshipped for its all-consuming energy, as it burns up one object after another, until nothing remains to be burnt. Surely, such worship amounts to nothing more than cultivating an attitude of untiring persistence, which never gives up in the face of trouble, as one difficulty succeeds another in the course of life.'

'I worship as the absolute that spirit which is seen in life-giving water.'

'It seems to me that water is worshipped for its accommodating fluidity, whereby it flows into shapes that accord with its surroundings. Surely, such worship amounts to nothing more than cultivating an attitude of graceful adaptation to changing circumstances.'

'I worship as the absolute that spirit of inward reflection which is embodied in a mirror.'

'It seems to me that this spirit of reflection is worshipped for its clarifying radiance, whereby it shines with light reflected from within. Surely, such worship amounts to nothing more than cultivating clarity of mind and purpose, whereby a person shines out among friends and associates.'

'I worship as the absolute that inner spirit of meaning which is expressed in living words and actions.'

'It seems to me that this spirit of meaning is worshipped as the subtle breath of life, whereby an otherwise merely physical action is infused with life and meaning. Surely, such worship amounts to nothing more than the cultivation of intellect and sensibility, by which we try to make the most of our limited personalities in this conditioned world.'

'I worship as the absolute that unifying spirit which reconciles different points of view.'

'It seems to me that this unifying spirit is worshipped for its construction of order and system, by which society and learning are co-ordinated. Surely, such worship amounts to no more than the cultivation of tolerance and understanding, so that people can come together for mutual support, across personal variations and differences.'

'I worship as the absolute that spirit which is seen in shadow and darkness.'

'It seems to me that this spirit of darkness is worshipped as the death of passing things. Surely, such worship amounts to nothing more than the cultivation of a full and unflinching life, through the inevitable deaths and destructions of the passing world.'

'I worship as the absolute that spirit which is seen in the living self of each individual person ... and, indeed, in the universal self of the entire world.'

'It seems to me that you are using the word "self" here to describe something seen. And thus, what you call "self" is worshipped as a personality that is made up of body and mind. Surely, such worship amounts to nothing more than the cultivation of personal powers of body and mind.'

After this last reply from Ajātashatru, Gārgya remained silent.

'Is this all?' asked Ajātashatru.

'Yes, it is all,' Gārgya replied.

'But it does not lead to the absolute,' said Ajātashatru.

'Then tell me what does,' said Gārgya, in a moment of humility.

'It isn't usual for a learned scholar to seek the highest knowledge from a warrior-king,' said Ajātashatru. 'But I shall tell you what I know.'

Then Ajātashatru got up and took Gārgya for a little walk, through the palace grounds. Walking together, they came upon a sleeping man. Ajātashatru called out to the sleeper, addressing him as the 'Great white-robed Soma, Lord of Dreams.' But this did not wake him, so Ajātashatru put out his hand and shook the sleeper until he awoke and rose up.

Ajātashatru said to Gārgya: 'Now that this man has been awakened, you see in him a manifestation of that underlying principle of consciousness which he shares in common with you and me and every other person. But where was this principle of consciousness during sleep? Where has it come from now?'

Gārgya could think of no reply.

Ajātashatru continued: 'When a person is awake, consciousness appears in the outgoing faculties of personality, in the five senses and in outward actions, through which attention is turned to the external world. But when a person falls asleep, awareness is withdrawn from these outgoing faculties; and consciousness remains within mind and heart, whose very essence it is.

'In the state of sleep, consciousness is evidently absorbed in itself. For in this state, all faculties of awareness have been drawn in. Vitality does not go outward in external action; meaning does not go outwards in speech or any other external expression; perception does not go outwards through the five senses; understanding does not go out towards the interpretation of external sensations; and the mind does not direct attention out to the external world.

'In dreams, a person may seem to be a powerful king or a learned scholar or to have attained some high or low position in life. But, whatever worlds a person may pass through in dream, these are but worlds of the dreamer's own consciousness. Just as a powerful king may take his retinue of followers and travel as he desires through his own country, so too a dreaming mind takes up its own internal faculties and moves as it desires through its own worlds of mental experience.

'And further, when a person enters into a state of deep sleep, the mind ceases to be aware of anything at all, as it returns along the multitude of channels that are said to branch out from within the heart. As the mind thus returns to its own centre, it comes to rest and dissolves entirely, in that underlying principle of consciousness which abides at the centre of each personality.

'Like an innocent child who hasn't a care in the world, or like some successful person who has achieved all that's desired, or like a discerning philosopher who rests content in the unqualified joy of plain truth; so too a person in deep sleep has come to the unconditioned happiness of pure peace, at that same centre of life which is each person's real self.

'By looking back to dreamless sleep
where dreams and waking thoughts arise,
one sees the depth of one's own self
from which the seeming world is known.

'At first this underlying depth
seems hidden in obscurity.
Dissolved in sleep, no feelings feel,
no thoughts conceive, no senses see
or hear or smell or taste or touch,
and no appearances appear.

'Here only darkness seems perceived.

'But darkness too is an appearance
that's perceived by sense and mind.
It too dissolves in depth of sleep;
it can't, in truth, be present here.

'When darkness too is known dissolved,
there's nothing left but consciousness:
not now reflected by appearances,
but shining by itself
as self-illuminating light.

'Our minds and senses only see
appearances reflecting light.
When they look back to light itself,
they are immediately dissolved
and can't see anything at all.

'Thus dazzled by the very light
of consciousness by which they see,
it seems to them dark nothingness,
wherever sight has been turned back
from seeming things to look at it.

'The seeming darkness of deep sleep
shows self, beneath all sense and mind,
as unconditioned consciousness:
where all the world dissolves in light.

'As a spider from its body
sends out threads and weaves a web,
or as small sparks come forth from fire;

'so too, from this same self come forth
all energies, all lives, all worlds,
all gods and all created things.

'This is that final teaching
which is said to be the "truth of truth".

'Truth is all things; and of all things, *from*
self is the truth of each.' *2.1*

Immanent and transcendent

Two aspects of reality
result in two opposing ways
through which it seems to be approached.

One aspect is its *immanence*:

as that which does not merely seem,
but really *is*, in seeming things;

as that which is invariant
through varying appearances;

as that which dying things express
by living till they die away;

as that embodied principle
within each body's changing acts.

But this same immanent reality,
existing here and now,
also *transcends* all seeming things:

as that transcendent principle
beyond all mere appearances;

as that which causes every change,
by going on through everything;

as that which does not suffer death,
while seeming things all die away;

as unconditioned consciousness, *from*
unmixed with body's seeming acts. *2.3.1*

Self and reality[4]

All creatures feed on fruit of earth;
and earth, in turn, is fed by them.

Both in earth and in each person,
that which shines and never dies
is our common 'human-ness'.

This is the self each person is.

It is that same reality
which always lives, unchanged, complete, *from*
in every partial-seeming thing. *2.5.1*

This self is lord and king of all.

As in a wheel, all spokes are joined
together at the hub and rim;
so too, all things, all gods, all worlds,
all lives, all separate-seeming selves *from*
are joined together in the self. *2.5.15*

This, which lives in all our bodies,
is our common 'human-ness'.

Outside this, there's no existence. *from*
Nothing is, apart from this. *2.5.18*

It is this that takes the likeness
of each form that is perceived.

From appearance thus created
come the many forms of God,
harnessing those many
different faculties of sense and action
which create our seeming world.

[4]See *Interpreting the Upanishads*, pages 95-98, for an indication of how this retelling interprets the original text.

All our senses, all our bodies,
all the many, countless things
they see and touch, are nothing but
this one same self in each of us.

It is that all-containing truth
with nothing else beside itself,
with nothing else before itself,
with nothing else that follows on,
with no outside and no inside.

Thus it is taught: *'This self is in*
itself complete. It knows all things, *from*
and all it knows is but itself.' *2.5.19*

A contest of learning[5]

Janaka, King of Videha, once performed a great sacrifice, at which much patronage was liberally distributed among the eminent men of learning who had travelled from their homes in many kingdoms to be present there. Curious to know who was the most learned among them, King Janaka assembled a herd of one thousand fine cattle, each with ten gold coins tied between the horns.

'Honoured Sirs,' he said to his illustrious guests, 'may these cattle be led away by the most learned among you.'

At first, no one responded and there was an awkward, hesitant silence. Then Yājnyavalkya said to one of his disciples: 'Gentle Sāmashravas, take charge of the cattle.' And Sāmashravas went forward to do so.

A wave of angry murmuring spread through the many other men of learning who were assembled there, for they felt: 'Who is he to claim more learning than the rest of us?'

The first to speak out was Ashvala, one of King Janaka's priests: 'Yājnyavalkya, how can you be so sure that you are more learned than everyone else who is present here?'

Yājnyavalkya replied: 'We all respect the most learned among scholars. We also all want the cattle.'

So Ashvala began his questioning: 'Yājnyavalkya, while all things in this world are caught up in death, and are overpowered by death, how can a worshipper transcend his own mortality?'

'Through the invoking priest, through fire and through speech,' Yājnyavalkya replied. 'Where the invoker, fire and speech are realized as one, there freedom is attained.'

'Yājnyavalkya, while all things in this world are caught up in the alternation of day and night, how can a worshipper transcend such passing periodicity?'

'Through the priest who sees to the ritual actions, through the sun and through sight. Where see-er, sun and sight are realized as one, there freedom is attained.'

[5]See *Interpreting the Upanishads*, pages 61-68, for an indication of how a part of this retelling interprets the original text (in particular 3.8.3-5,7-11, where Gārgī questions Yājnyavalkya a second time).

'Yājnyavalkya, while all things in this world are caught up in the waxing and waning of the moon, how can a worshipper transcend such tides of time?'

'Through the chanting priest, through the air and through the breath of life. Where chanter, air and life are realized as one, there freedom is attained.'

'Yājnyavalkya, given that the sky seems to be held aloft without support, through what means of ascent may heaven be attained?'

'Through the supervising priest, through the moon and through thought. Where supervisor, moon and thought are realized as one, there freedom is attained.'

Thus Yājnyavalkya answered questions from Ashvala and from many others. At first, preliminary questions were asked, about ritual and cosmic symbols and about personality and mind. Then Ushasta, son of Cakra, began to question Yājnyavalkya about the absolute.

'Yājnyavalkya, can you explain the nature of that all-comprehending reality which is immediately present and directly known, as the universal self in everything?'

'This reality is your own self,' said Yājnyavalkya. 'Your own self, just as you really are, is there in everything.'

'But *what* is it, in everything?'

'It is life, in living actions,
life drawn back in rest and peace,
life pervading different actions,
life raised up in happiness.

'This is your self, in everything.'

'But Yājnyavalkya, by describing the absolute as "life", you are only indicating that we might look for it in the outward manifestations of life: as for example in a horse or a cow, for these are both forms of life. What is the absolute *in itself*?'

'The seeing principle
that sees all sights
cannot be seen.

'The hearing principle
that hears all sounds
cannot be heard.

'The thinking principle
that shines as meaning
in all thought
cannot be thought.

'The knowing principle
that knows all knowledge
can't be known
by body, sense or mind.

'This is your self, in everything.
All else is misery and wrong.'

Ushasta was satisfied, and held his peace.

But Kahola, son of Kushītaka, did not quite understand what Yājnyavalkya had said; and so he persisted with the same question: 'Yājnyavalkya, could you further explain to me the nature of this absolute reality which is always immediately present and directly known, as the universal self of everything?'

'This reality is your own individual self. Your own individual self is always present, here and now, in everything.'

'But what *is* it, in everything?'

'It is beyond hunger and thirst, beyond grief and delusion, beyond decay and death. Realizing this self, men of knowledge rise above desire for family and wealth and worlds. And thus, they are naturally freed from the bondage of petty desires for the limited, passing objects of the apparent world. For they come to understand that all desires for objects are only varying manifestations of longing for the true happiness of unconditioned self.

'A man of learning who has had enough of technical sophistication may seek a life of innocence and simplicity. When he has also had enough of innocence and simplicity, he may become contemplative. When he has had enough of contemplation and states beyond contemplation, then he may become a true man of knowledge.'

'How may such a man of knowledge be?'

'However he may seem to be, in that he is true to knowledge. All else is misery and wrong.'

And now Kahola held his peace.

Then Gārgī, daughter of Vacaknu, asked: 'Yājnyavalkya, what common basis can be found to underlie the different objects of the world?'

'The different objects of the world are said to arise from the element called "earth". This is the element of apparent solidity in the world, whereby each object has a separate identity of its own, separated from the rest of the world by recognizable boundaries in space and time. As clay is fashioned into different pots, so also all the different objects of the world are fashioned from the element called "earth".'

'But, on what basis do different objects come to acquire their separate identities?'

'The separate identity of each "earth"-born object arises from its form, by which its parts are related together in a particular fashion that makes the object recognizable as a distinct entity. And this relationship of parts is a product of the transformations that have fashioned the object and have brought it into manifest existence. Thus, the separate identity of "earth"-born objects is fashioned on the basis of a further element called "water", the fluid element of form and transformation. And, from this, it may be seen that the solid element, "earth", is permeated by its underlying basis in "water", the fluid element of changing form.'

'But then, what is the basis of this fluid element, called "water"?'

'The illuminating element of meaning, called "fire". For it is on the basis of meaning that the changing forms of the world are known, as they shine with light from understanding.'

'And what is the basis of this meaningful element, called "fire"?'

'The element of quality, called "air", which is not seen by the gross senses, but is more subtly felt by intuition and sensibility. For it is on the basis of their qualities that forms are able to express meaning.'

'And what is the basis of this qualitative element, called "air"?'

'The element of continuity, called "ether", which pervades the differing objects, forms, meanings and qualities that are perceived in the apparent world. For it is on the basis of continuing principles that differing objects and their varying forms, meanings and qualities are related, compared and understood: as differing manifestations of common reality.'

'And what is the basis of this continuing, pervasive element, called "ether"?'

'The subtle worlds of celestial spirits, who live in the ethereal regions of the sky.'

'And what is the basis of these celestial worlds?'

'The worlds of radiant sun, above the sky.'

'And what is the basis of these worlds of sun?'

'The worlds of moon and stars, whose light shines when the sun has set.'

'And what is the basis of these worlds of moon and stars?'

'The worlds of gods, who govern the stars, the moon, the sun, the sky, and all the elements.'

'And what is the basis of these worlds of gods?'

'The worlds of Indra, Lord of gods, who rules the other gods.'

'And what is the basis of these worlds of Indra, Lord of gods?'

'The worlds of God the Creator, from whom all gods and all things else are born.'

'And what is the basis of these worlds of God the Creator?'

'The great totality of all existence, called "brahman", which includes all things.'

'And what about this all-including totality, called "brahman"?'

'At this point, Gārgī, your questioning is on the verge of becoming idle; and your reasoning is about to defeat itself. The great totality called "brahman" is the basis of all things, including reason and all its questionings. In order to find this great totality, reason must dig up the ground from under its own feet; and thus it must be absorbed and must dissolve into its own basis. There, it is meaningless to imagine any remaining faculty of reason that asks questions about some further basis.'

Gārgī had to accept that she had come to the end of this particular line of reasoning. And so, for the time being, she remained silent.

Next, it was Uddālaka, son of Aruṇa, who took up the questioning: 'Yājnyavalkya, when my fellow students and I were studying sacrificial ritual under Patancala Kāpya of the Madra tribe, his wife was possessed by a celestial spirit. The spirit told us he was Kabandha, son of Atharvan, and he asked two questions:

'"Do you know that thread by which all beings, all this world and any other worlds are strung together?

'"And do you know that inner controller who controls all beings, all this world and any other worlds?"

'Our teacher said he did not know.

'The spirit said: "By knowing this thread and this inner controller, a person comes to knowledge of the absolute ... of worlds, gods, scriptures, living beings, self, and everything."

'Yājnyavalkya, do you know this thread and inner controller? If you do not, and if you still take these cows that have been dedicated to a knower of the absolute, then you will surely come to grief.'

'Yes, I know the thread and the inner controller.'

'Anyone can say: "I know, I know." Tell us what you know.'

'The thread you speak of is the subtle breath of life, which is manifested in the meaningful coherence that we find expressed in the functioning of the universe. By this thread of living breath, all beings, all the world and any other worlds are strung together. Thus, when a person dies, the body's parts are no longer held together in meaningful coherence by living breath, and they are easily dispersed as lifeless earth.'

'Yes, it is so. Now tell us of the inner controller.'

'It is that inner principle
there in the earth, unknown by earth,
controlling earth as its own body.

'It is the inner principle
of waters, fire, air and ether,
sky and sun and moon and stars.

'It is the inner principle
of light and dark, and living things,
of living faculties and sense,
of mind and heart and consciousness.

'Never seen, it is the see-er;
never heard, it is the hearer;
never thought, it is the thinker;
never known, it is the knower.

'Nothing else can see or hear
or think or feel or understand.
Nothing else can know at all.

'This is the inner controller.
It is your self, your very own;
and it is never touched by death.
All else is misery and wrong.'

Uddālaka was satisfied, and held his peace.

Now Gārgī spoke again: 'Yājnyavalkya, I have two further questions for you. They are all that I can ask.'

'Yes, Gārgī. Ask.'

'Yājnyavalkya, when I was questioning you a short while ago, we proceeded along a tortuous path of cosmic elements and gods. Let me now try to proceed more directly. What is the substance of all that is said to be existence: above heaven, below earth, in earth and heaven and in between, in all that was and is and is to be?'

'This all-pervasive substance is called "ether". It is not a gross substance, like "earth", which can be fashioned into separate objects, as a potter fashions clay into pots. Instead, this "ether" is the highly subtle substance of underlying continuity: which enables each object or event to be understood, in relation to other objects and events located elsewhere in space and time.

'Through the limited perceptions of body, senses and mind, limited objects and events appear at the forefront of attention. Each particular object or event is thus a limited and partial appearance of a much larger world. Each such limited appearance, of only one particular object or event, is understood in relation to a background of experience which somehow comprehends other objects and events that are not explicitly seen or thought of at the time.

'As attention turns from one appearance to another, the background of experience continues, enabling different appearances and different objects and events to be related. In every object or event that appears in experience, this continuing background is understood. Its continuity thus extends throughout experience: through all space and time, through all relationships and through all causes and effects.

'The subtle substance "ether" is essentially unmanifest. Unlike gross matter, it is not manifested by its separation into different objects and events. Instead, it underlies experience, as the continuing background that is implicitly understood in the perception of all objects and events. It is the continuing background of the entire world: the complete background of all-containing space, time and causality.'

'Yes, this is a satisfying answer, and it leads to my second question. On what basis does this continuing background pervade all of existence?'

'The basis of all space, all time,
all cause, cannot itself be changed,
nor qualified, by changing
qualities of space and time and cause.
Thus, it is described as "changeless".

'It is not coarse, nor yet refined;
it is not long or short, nor wet
or dry; nor has it colour,
shade or darkness, taste or smell.

'It is not "air", nor "ether":
for it has no qualities,
and it cannot be related
to anything besides itself.

'It has no eyes, no ears, no speech,
no mind; it is not sharp, nor has
it vital force, nor face, nor measure.
Nor does it consume, nor is consumed.
It has no outside, nor inside.

'Based on this changeless principle,
the sun and moon are kept on course,
and heaven and earth remain in place.

'Moments pass in due succession,
days give way to nights and nights to days,
seasons alternate and years pass by.
Rivers rise and flow from mountains.
People work to seek reward.

'Wherever there is ignorance
of this one changeless principle,
work but results in passing gain.

'To leave the world in ignorance
of changeless truth is misery.

'But one who knows this changeless truth
has reached the goal of all desire,
and leaves the world in deathless peace
with nothing further to attain.

'This changeless principle
cannot be seen:
it is the see-er.

'It can't be heard:
it is the hearer.

'It can't be thought:
it is the thinker.

'It can't be known:
it is the knower.

'Nothing else can see or hear
or think or feel or understand.

'Nothing else can know at all.

'Gārgī, this changeless, knowing principle is the basis on which stands the all-pervading continuity called "ether". This is the ultimate basis of all apparent existence.'

Now Gārgī turned to the learned assembly of her fellow priests and scholars. 'Honoured Sirs,' she said, 'you should consider yourselves lucky if you can get away from him by paying nothing more than your respects. I cannot see how any of you will ever defeat him in exposition of the absolute.'

Then Vidagdha, son of Shakala, asked: 'Yājnyavalkya, how many gods are there?'

'As stated in the invocation to the gods: three hundred and three, and three thousand and three.'

'So it is said. But, more correctly, how many gods are there?'

'Thirty-three.'

'So it is said. But, more correctly, how many gods are there?'

'Six.'

'So it is said. But, more correctly, how many gods are there?'

'Three.'

'So it is said. But, more correctly, how many gods are there?'

'Two.'

'So it is said. But, more correctly, how many gods are there?'

'One and a half.'

'So it is said. But, more correctly, how many gods are there?'

'One.'

'So it is said. But tell us, who are all these gods?'

'In effect, there are only thirty-three gods. The others are their manifestations.'

'Which are these thirty-three?'

'Eight gods that shine; eleven gods that wail; twelve gods that take away. And further, the Lord of gods and God the Creator.'

'Which are the gods that shine?'

'Fire, earth, air, sky, the sun, the heavens, the moon and the stars. All things are guided by these shining gods.'

'Which are the gods that wail?'

'A person has five faculties of sense: sight, sound, smell, taste and touch. So also there are five faculties of action: expression, represented by the spoken voice; acquisition, represented by a person's grasping hands; locomotion, represented by a person's walking feet; expulsion, represented by the discharge of bodily waste; and regeneration, represented by the birth and bringing up of children. In addition to these ten faculties of sense and action, there is the inner faculty of mind; making eleven faculties in all. These eleven faculties are gods that wail, because they herald pain and misery, as they go out to an external world of conflict and destruction.'

'Which are the gods that take away?'

'The twelve months of the year, which represent the passing of time. As time passes, it takes all things away.'

'Who is the Lord of gods, and who is the Creator?'

'The Lord of gods is represented by the thunder-cloud, and the Creator is represented by the ritual of sacrifice.'

'How does the thunder-cloud represent the Lord of gods?'

'Through the brilliance of concentrated energy, in lightning.'

'How is the Creator represented in the ritual of sacrifice?'

'Through the regeneration of life, in sacrificing the gross and subtle bodies.'

'How then can all these gods be reduced to six?'

'All of them may be reduced to fire, earth, air, the sky, the sun and the heavens. For, through these six gods of light and space, all other gods are known.'

'And how may the gods be reduced further, to three?'

'The world of earth consists of earth and fire. The world of sky consists of sky and air. The world of heaven consists of the heavens and the sun. Thus, these three worlds encompass all the gods.'

'And how may this further be reduced to two?'

'If we consider all the matter in the earth and sky and heavens, and if we consider all the energy in fire and air and sun; then all gods are reduced to matter and energy.'

'And how may this be further reduced, to one and a half?'

'The subtle breath of life, which is manifested in all the functioning of matter and energy, is one and a half.'

'Why is it one and a half?'

'Because all things appear through its manifesting energy, thus giving it an extra half existence: the extra half existence of partial manifestation, which it appears to possess, in addition to its own proper existence.'

'Then how can there be one God, alone?'

'That one God is life itself, unconditioned and unmanifest. It is the absolute, besides which nothing else exists. It is called merely: "That".'

'Yājnyavalkya, you have out-argued other men of learning by your claim to know the absolute. But, *what* do you know about it?'

'I know how the absolute may be represented in various directions, through various deities and the supporting foundations on which they depend.'

'In that case, what is the deity of the east?'

'The sun.'

'On what does this deity depend?'

'On sight.'

'On what does sight depend?'

'On the visual forms and qualities that are seen by sight.'

'On what do these forms and qualities depend?'

'On the heart, for forms and qualities are known and understood through the intuition of the heart.'

'Very well, but what is the deity of the south?'

'Death.'

'On what does this deity of death depend?'

'On sacrifice.'

'On what does sacrifice depend?'

'On offering.'

'On what does offering depend?'

'On faith. For offerings are made when there is faith.'

'On what does faith depend?'

'On the heart. For faith arises from the judgement of the heart.'

'Very well. But what is the deity of the west?'

'Rain.'

'On what does this deity depend?'

'On water.'

'On what does water depend?'

'On the fertility of creation.'

'On what does fertility depend?'

'On the heart. For creation grows from seeds of thought and feeling that emerge from the heart, as a child grows from its parents' seed.'

'Very well, but what is the deity of the north?'

'The moon, god of mystery and imagination.'

'On what does this deity depend?'

'On initiation.'

'On what does initiation depend?'

'On truth, as when an initiate is enjoined to speak the truth.'

'On what does truth depend?'

'On the heart. For truth is known through purity of heart.'

'Very well, but what is the deity of the upward direction, towards the zenith overhead?'

'Fire.'

'On what does this deity depend?'

'On the meaningful expression of knowledge, as exemplified by speech.'

'On what does meaningful expression depend?'

'On the heart.'

'On what does the heart depend?'

'Now you have asked a foolish question,' said Yājnyavalkya. 'If you think that your heart can be anything apart from your self, then you become a ghost: an empty shell of mere appearance which must disappear when properly examined in the sober light of day. Devoid of living self, there is no heart; and the body is nothing more than dead meat, fit to be eaten by dogs or torn apart by vultures.'

'Since you make out that you are so clever, on what do you and your precious "self" depend?'

'In each person's body, an appearance of self is created by the outgoing faculty of expression, which is projected from within the heart towards the external world.'

'On what does this outgoing faculty depend?'

'On the in-drawing faculty of observation, which takes perception into the mind.'

'On what does this in-drawing faculty depend?'

'On the discerning faculty of interpretation, which reflects back and forth between observation and understanding, thus interpreting the meaning of perceptions.'

'On what does this discerning faculty depend?'

'On the integrating faculty of understanding, which assimilates meaning into the heart, and which co-ordinates expression as it is projected outwards from the heart.'

Vidagdha remained silent now; so Yājnyavalkya continued: 'But surely, the enquiry doesn't end here. A further question remains to be asked. What is that fundamental principle from which all experience is projected, and into which all perception and meaning are assimilated?'

Vidagdha was quite out of his depth, and could not answer. His reason clouded over and his manner became strangely awkward, as though his limbs and faculties no longer quite belonged to him. For it had turned out that he did not properly understand his own arguments, and he could no longer tell quite what to think or say.

Then Yājnyavalkya said: 'Honoured priests and scholars, do any of you wish to question me further? Or are there any of you who would be questioned by me?'

No one spoke out in reply, so Yājnyavalkya continued: 'Then I will put a question to all of you together.

'A tree that's cut sprouts up again
from root, and thus it is reborn.
But if a tree is pulled up
by the roots, it is not born again.

'A person is not born just once,
for personality is changed;
each passing moment of our lives.
Each moment, we are born again.

'What is the root from which a person
is reborn, time after time?

'What is the ground which holds the root,
the ground in which all life dissolves
each time it dies and is reborn,
the ground in which life comes to peace
when the root has been pulled out?'

Again, no one answered. So Yājnyavalkya said:

'The root is ego's ignorance,
falsely identifying self
as changing personality:
as little body, born of flesh,
or senses going out to world,
or shifting mind that dies away
with every thought that passes on.

'The ground is what self really is,
continuing through seeming change:
the source and goal of everything,
pure knowledge, unmixed happiness.'

from chapter 3

Light [6]

One day, on a visit to King Janaka, Yājnyavalkya remained silent. So Janaka asked:

'Yājnyavalkya, what is light?'

'Light is the radiance of the sun,
by which each person sees a world
of sights and shapes and moving things,
a world of colours, contrasts, shades.

'By light a person sees a world
outside, goes out into this world
to get things done, and comes back home.'

'But Yājnyavalkya, when the sun
has set and night has come, what then
is light that shows us what we see?'

'Light is the radiance of the moon,
by which a person sees the world
at night, goes out into this world
to get things done, and comes back home.'

'But Yājnyavalkya, when both moon
and sun have vanished from the sky,
what then is light by which we see?'

'When both the sun and moon have vanished,
light shines out from burning fire.
Thus, even on a moonless night
a person sees the world, goes out
to get things done, and comes back home.'

'But Yājnyavalkya, what is light
when fire is burnt out and shines
no more, so eyes no longer see?'

[6]See *Interpreting the Upanishads*, pages 69-76, 166-167 and 171-172, for an indication of how parts of this retelling interpret the original text (in particular: 4.3.7-12,15-17 together with 4.4.16-22; 4.3.21; and 4.3.32; respectively).

'Then sight gives way to sound and smell
and taste and touch; for by such light
of other senses even those
who have no eyes observe the world,
go get things done, and come back home.'

'But Yājnyavalkya, in a dream
or deep in thought, when outward sense
has turned back in, when outward sight
and sound and smell and taste and touch
have disappeared, what then is light?'

'Then thought and feeling shine with light
by which each person knows the world,
goes out, does things, and comes back home.'

'But Yājnyavalkya, when the mind
is stilled, in dreamless sleep or in
deep meditation or between
successive thoughts, what is light then?'

'Then light is shown for what it is,
unmixed with falsities of mind.

'Light is the nature of the self;
for it is by the consciousness of
knowing self that everyone
makes observations, goes about *from*
the world, does things, and comes back home.' *4.3.1-6*

'But then, what is this knowing self?'

'It is the light of consciousness
within each living creature's heart.

'And though it seems to journey through
a waking world of outside things
or inner worlds of dreaming mind,

'in truth, it always stays the same
through all appearances of change.

'In depth of sleep, the self is shown *from*
beyond all worlds of changing form. *4.3.7*

'Where this self seems born as body,
it seems to suffer body's ills.
Each body dies, all ills must pass; *from*
that which remains, unchanged, is self. *4.3.8*

'There are two seeming states of self:

'as body in an outside world;

'or mind, conceiving subtle worlds
made up of its own thoughts and dreams.

'But, joining these apparent states,
is that third state where seeming stops,
where thoughts and dreams have all dissolved
and no appearances remain.

'This is the state of dreamless sleep;
the timeless state that is achieved
when meditation stills the mind;
the state between successive thoughts,
where previous thought has come to end
and further thought has not begun.

'Here, in this unconditioned state,
self shines unmixed with alien things
that make it seem what it is not.

'Remaining always in this state
of unconditioned purity,
self lights the body's waking world
and worlds of mind that dreaming brings.

'Whatever state seems to appear,
all seeming ills and seeming joys
are lit and known by self alone.

'As mind withdraws from world in sleep,
the whole created world dissolves
in all creation's shining source: *from*
where self is light which lights itself. *4.3.9*

'Here, where all dreams dissolve in light
from which they come, there is no change,
nor cause of change, nor place for change.
There is no need for fancy's flight, *from*
there are no bounds, there is no pain. *4.3.10*

'When body sleeps, the body's world
dissolves in unmixed consciousness;
as body's seeming consciousness
returns again to its true source
in that unsleeping, deathless self *from*
which knows all worlds, all dreams, all sleep. *4.3.11*

'The body's seeming life is bound
to breath, to circulating blood,
to many other vital needs
that keep our bodies functioning.

'But self is free, it has no needs;
it is untouched by seeming change.
As life itself, it cannot die.

'Through passing states of wakefulness
and dream and sleep, the self alone *from*
goes on from state to state, unchanged. *4.3.12*

'The wandering mind creates in dream
a multitude of passing forms.
It sometimes seems to laugh and play
in company of pleasant friends.
It sometimes seems beset by fear, *from*
caught up in pain and misery. *4.3.13*

'All this is but a fancied game
created by our seeming minds.
These minds, caught up in their own game,
don't see the source from which they come,
where fancies rise and come to rest.

'The waking state too can be seen
as but a dream of fancied thought.
There is no light outside the self, *from*
this self which is itself pure light. *4.3.14*

'In sleep, in dreams, in wakefulness,
the self is always free: unchanged
by all the good and evil things
that seem to pass before its light.

'It only knows, it does not act; *from*
and so it cannot be attached. *4.3.15-17*

'Through subtle tricks of seeming mind,
it may be ignorantly thought
that self is in a fallen state,
in bondage to an alien world.
But, when mind clears and comes to peace,
both self and world are seen as one.

'When this plain truth is understood,
all misery comes to an end
and all desire is realized;
for every object of desire
is known as nothing else but self.

'Self knows all things as consciousness,
and consciousness is merely self.
Self knows, but there is nothing else
for self to know. All knowledge is
no more or less than deathless self,
which shines with light that is itself.

'Self *is*, complete; because it *knows*,
and all it knows is self alone.'

'Then Yājnyavalkya, what is love
that makes a person feel the need
for unity with someone else?'

'When unity has been achieved
with someone who is truly loved,
all care dissolves in love itself,
which shines as peace and happiness.

'Thus, happiness of love attained
shows self and world as really one, *from*
beyond all false duality. *4.3.20-21*

'In this true non-duality,
there is no world outside the self.

'A mother is none else than self;
a father is none else than self.

'A thief is nothing else than self;
a murderer is only self.

'All gods and demons are but self.

'Self is beyond all good and ill, *from*
untouched by seeming loss and gain. *4.3.22*

'All that is seen is self alone.
All that is heard is self alone.
All that is smelled, or tasted, touched,
or spoken of, or thought, or felt,
is nothing else but self alone.

'In each sensation, each perception,
every thought and every feeling,
self is that which only knows:
unmixed with any kind of act.

'It sees, without an act of seeing
visualizing something else.
It hears without an act of hearing
listening to something else.

'It senses odour as mere smell:
as nothing else but consciousness,
not as the object of an act.

'It tastes, but all it tastes is flavour:
nothing else but consciousness,
not any object of an act.

'It touches all, but in this touching
stays unmoved and does not act.
It does not go from "this" to "that",
but just remains exactly what
it always is: pure consciousness.

'It speaks, without an act of speaking
saying words that represent
something else besides itself.

'It thinks, without mind's outward acts:
which start from mind and then go on
to something that is thought about.

'It thinks, without the mind's reflective
act: of thinking that it thinks,
and falling back into itself.

'It feels, without an act of feeling
going out to something else
and judging value in the world.

'It feels, without an act of feeling
changing from one state of mind
to another state of mind
that's brought about by mind's own actions
and by changing circumstance.

'In all that self experiences,
it never puts on any act
that starts from "this" and ends with "that".

'For there is nothing else to see
or hear or smell or taste or touch
or speak about or think or feel.

'There's nothing else but self alone.

from 4.3.23-31

'As all waves are only water,
so all seeming things are self,
which knows all things as but itself, *from*
as undivided happiness.' *4.3.32*

'But Yājnyavalkya, where is self
when body perishes at death?'

'Change and death pertain to body;
they never can pertain to self.
Though body changes, self remains;
though body dies, the self lives on.

'Thus self, continuing unchanged,
seems to move on from change to change,
sees to live on from birth to death,
from death to birth and death again.

'In truth, the self is life itself, *from*
where death and time do not arise. *4.3.35*
It cannot die or move or change. *–4.4.4*

'The self in every one of us
is all there is, all there can be.
But this completeness is obscured
by ego's false identity:
as self confused with partial things.

'Thus, self appears as feeling heart,
or thinking mind, or guiding will,
or senses that perceive a world,
or body acting in the world:
bound by the world, by likes, dislikes,
by forms and meanings, good and ill.

'Where self and body are confused,
a person seems to reap the fruit
of actions that are good or bad.
Good actions lead to benefit;
bad actions lead to loss and ill.

'Gross body's acts show mind's desire;
and thus the body's outward acts
show subtle mind, which thinks and feels *from*
and reaps the fruits of its desires. *4.4.5*

'By desire for outward objects,
mind is bound to outward acts.
But when desires are fulfilled
and turn back in, towards the self,
all bonds dissolve and self shines out
as free, unbounded consciousness.

'All that is sought in happiness
is just the nature of the self.'

'But Yājnyavalkya, happiness
seems to be just a passing state
of fickle, oscillating mind,
which rises up to heights of joy
and falls to depths of misery.

'With states of joy but short relief
from bondage to repeated grief,
how then can anyone break free
to lasting peace and happiness?'

'Whoever lusts for passing things
must suffer seeming loss and grief,
as objects that seem loved pass on.

'Whoever's heart is free from lust
knows here and now that self alone *from*
is source and goal of all desire. *4.4.6*

'As when a snake casts off its skin;
so too this seeming shell of mind
and body is cast off unmourned,
when self is known for what it is.

'Whoever realizes self
as deathless light, lives here and now
in lasting peace and happiness.
This is the way to deathlessness,
which everyone has always sought.

'By realizing what self is,
all bonds are loosed, all conflicts end,
all pain burns up, no faults remain.
All imperfections are dissolved *from*
in truth, as freedom is attained. *4.4.7-9*

'Lack of learning leads to blindness;
pretended learning leads to worse.
Unknowing, unenlightened life *from*
seems caught in death and joylessness. *4.4.10-11*

'When self is known for what it is,
how can the body's ills cause grief?
For self remains untouched, unbound,
the unaffected depth within *from*
our bodily uncertainties. *4.4.12*

'Whoever knows and understands
this real self gains all the world, *from*
for all the world is but this self. *4.4.13*

'The truth is here before our eyes:
it's ours to understand right now.
If not, we suffer misery.

'Those who are ignorant find loss; *from*
those who know truth find deathlessness. *4.4.14*

'When self is seen to be the source
of all we seek or need or wish,
transcending all that was or is
or ever shall in future be,
no reason can be left to shrink *from*
from facing plain reality. *4.4.15*

'Before the self, all moments pass,
each day proceeds and turns to night,
each season gives way to the next,
and seasons cycle into years.

'For self is knowing consciousness,
which knows all time, all place, all things.
It is the ever-present light *from*
that lights all lights in all we know. *4.4.16*

'Through all appearances that come
and go in our experience,
this knowing consciousness goes on
from difference to difference,
from change to change. And through all change
it is the vital core of life,
which lasts, as all else comes and goes.

'This never-changing consciousness
is that immortal absolute
upon which all experience rests. *from*
Just knowing it brings deathlessness. *4.4.17*

'It is the living principle
in all the various lives we lead.
It is the seeing principle
in all the various sights we see.
It is the hearing principle
in all appearances of sound.

'It is the knowing principle
in all our minds' experiences:
in all the meanings we perceive,
in all the various thoughts we think, *from*
in all the feelings that we feel. *4.4.18*

'But, in this knowing principle,
which knows all change and difference,
no change or difference exists.

'Whoever sees diversity
and change sees but appearances, *from*
which only lead from death to death. *4.4.19*

'Self is that one unchanging truth
which can't be known by changing mind.

'Shared in common by all difference,
stainless through all imperfection,
never born in all creation,
limitless through space and time;
beyond all words, beyond all thought,
beyond all forms and qualities;

'self is known by simply being, *from*
because its nature is to shine. *4.4.20-21*

'True self is unborn consciousness,
the ground of all experience,
from which appearances are born.

'It is life in living function,
source and aim of all intention,
untouched depth of all emotion,
infinite, within each heart.

'No action can affect this self:
good actions cannot make it grow,
bad actions cannot cause it loss.
It is complete reality,
beyond all partial-seeming things.

'It is the underlying ground
from which all difference seems to rise,
on which all different things seem to
exist apart, to which all
seeming difference must return again.

'It is the final goal we seek,
through learning, love and sacrifice.

'Those who renounce the world's desires,
and wander far in search of truth,
find what they seek when they find self.

'It is described by negatives,
as truth which is "not this, not that";
for it is nothing limited
which mind or body can perceive.

'Unperceived by partial senses,
self can never be obstructed,
can't be bound like mind and body,
can't be fooled by lying ego *from*
making self seem incomplete. *4.4.22*

'Whoever truly finds the self
transcends all ego's petty sense
of seeming, partial separateness.

'All ills burn up, all bonds are freed;
all strife, all doubts give way to peace *from*
of deathless truth that never ends.' *4.4.23-25*

A last settlement[7]

Yājnyavalkya had two wives, Maitreyī and Kātyāyanī. Of the two, Maitreyī was interested in questions of ultimate truth. When the time came for Yājnyavalkya to renounce the life of a householder, he said: 'Maitreyī, I must leave. Let me make a last settlement upon you and Kātyāyanī.'

Maitreyī replied: 'If this whole world and all its wealth were mine, would that make me deathless?'

'No,' said Yājnyavalkya, 'you would then lead the life of the wealthy. But you cannot hope to find deathlessness in wealth.'

Maitreyī said: 'What should I do with things that do not lead to deathlessness? All I ask is that you teach me what you know.'

Yājnyavalkya replied: 'You have always been very dear to me, and what you say now makes you dearer still. Yes, if you like, I shall teach you. But you will have to think hard about it.

'What does a wife love in her husband?
Is it just that he's a husband?
If it's that, it isn't love.
All she can love in him is self.

'And when a husband loves his wife,
is it love if she's just a wife?
All he can love in her is self.

'So also love of children, friends,
living creatures, places, objects,
love of power, love of knowledge.
All that's loved is only self.

'When this self is seen and known,
then all the world is truly known *from*
and there is nothing else to know. *4.5.1-6*

[7]See *Interpreting the Upanishads*, pages 164-166 and 11-20, for an indication of how parts of this retelling interpret the original text (in particular: 4.5.6-7 and 4.5.13-15, respectively).

'Where learning is not realized
as self, such learning cannot last.
Where power is not realized
as self, nor can such power stay.

'Where worlds or gods or living things
or any other things are not
realized as self; such alien things
must part from self in course of time,
must be obscured and disappear,
must seem unstable, seem unsure,
must seem to change and pass away.

'In truth all learning, power, worlds,
gods, living things and all things else
are nothing other than the self. *from 4.5.7*

'Just as sounds of drum-beats, fanfare
and plucked strings are understood
only as music that expresses
meaning from the player's self;

'just as fire when it burns
produces different kinds of smoke;

'so also, different kinds of
scripture, verses, aphorisms,
explanations, sacrifice,
this world, the next, all life
and all apparent things are
but the breath of this great being. *from 4.5.8-11*

'Like waters merging in the sea,
all colours merge in sense of sight,
sounds are merged in sense of hearing,
odours merge in sense of smell,
flavours merge in sense of taste,
felt sensations merge in touch;

'actions merge in motivation,
all expressions merge in meaning,
thoughts and ideas merge in mind,
and feelings are all merged in heart. *from 4.5.12*

'Salt that is dissolved in water
cannot be picked out by fingers,
can't be held by grasping hands.
It's not a separate lump of salt;
it has no outside nor inside.

'But it is there in every drop,
for each drop tastes of saltiness.

'So too, the self is everywhere;
though it can't be picked out by senses,
cannot be conceived by mind.
It's not a bounded piece of world;
it has no outside nor inside.

'But it's here, in all experience,
always here, as consciousness.

'All mind and sense, and all the objects
they perceive, are formed from changing
elements; in course of time,
they all must change and pass away.

'Wherever knowledge is attained,
no such perception can remain.'

At this point, Yājnyavalkya paused, with the remark: 'Well, that's what I say.'

Maitreyī said: 'Just here, I am confused. Where knowledge is attained, how does perception cease? I can't make sense of it.'

Yājnyavalkya replied: 'It isn't really confusing, if you distinguish the changing perception of apparent objects from the continuing basis of consciousness into which each perception is absorbed.

'As perceptions are absorbed,
they're known as mere appearances
produced by acts of sense and mind
that part reveal and part conceal
the nature of reality.
Thus understood, they are dissolved
in underlying consciousness.

'And consciousness is that which knows
appearances, as mind and sense
perceive a world of changing things.

'But no appearance can exist
apart from knowing consciousness.
Any appearance that departs
from consciousness must disappear
at once, and is no longer there.

'Thus, no appearance has any
existence outside consciousness;
and all of the reality
that each appearance truly shows
is nothing else but consciousness.

'As consciousness illuminates
appearances of seeming world,
in truth, it only knows itself.

'In it, there's no duality
of knowing self and object known.
It is at once the self that knows
and all that's ever really known.

'Duality seems to arise
where it appears that something sees
or hears or smells or tastes or touches
something else besides itself;

'or where it seems that something
speaks about or thinks about or knows
some object other than itself.

'But when all things are realized
as nothing else but self alone,
by whom can what be seen? By whom
can what be heard, smelled, tasted, touched,
described, conceived, desired and known?

'By whom is knowledge truly known?

'The knowing self cannot be any
kind of object in the world.

'Not this, nor that, nor here, nor there
in space or time, it never can
be anything perceived through any
faculty of any body
or of any sense or mind.

'It is unowned, can't be possessed;
it does not die, does not decay,
is unattached, cannot be bound
or limited or qualified;
nor can it ever suffer harm
or be disturbed in any way.

'Thus, deathlessness may be attained
by asking, till no lies remain:

'"*How can the self that knows be known?*"

'Maitreyī, this is the instruction that you asked. Such is the way to deathlessness.'

With these words, Yājnyavalkya left home. *from 4.5.13-15*

The essence of personality[8]

The essence of this personality
that seems to rise from mind
is nothing else but light itself,
found here within each person's heart;

just as the essence of a plant
that seems to rise and grow from seed
is nothing else but life itself,
somehow contained within each seed.

This inner principle of light
guides all experience, and hence governs
everything that we perceive, *from*
beneath whatever seems to be. *5.6.1*

[8]See *Interpreting the Upanishads*, page 106, for an indication of how this retelling interprets the original text.

From the Chāndogya Upanishad

Change and space [1]

What is this change and movement
that appears to form our world?

All seeming motion is but space;
for everything is formed in space.
When formed, each thing is part of space;
whatever moves, must move in space.
Contained in space, all forms arise
and move and change and pass away.

All moving things and changing forms
arise, take shape, continue on
and come to end in space alone.

from 1.9.1

[1]The word 'space' here translates 'ākāsha', which also means 'ether' or 'sky'. The underlying sense is that of pervasiveness and continuation. Accordingly, 'space' is not here conceived in a narrow sense: as the distance that *separates* particular objects. Instead, it is conceived in a more universal sense: as *continuing* space and time, which together contain the entire universe, and which thus *connect* different objects. In this conception, all of space and time are taken together, as the pervasive and unifying background of the world, in which each physical and mental thing must be located.

There is a striking correspondence here with modern physics. In the theory of relativity, Einstein conceived the physical world as a 'space-time continuum': where space, time, matter and energy are essentially inter-related and must be considered together, in order to understand an invariant and continuing reality beneath the variations and changes of relative appearance.

See *Interpreting the Upanishads*, pages 60-61, for a further indication of how this retelling interprets the original text.

Personality and consciousness

The living core of consciousness
within each personality
is greater than all outward acts.

The changing world of partial things
and all appearances of mind
are seeming parts of consciousness.

The greater, truer part is that
illuminating principle
which lights up all appearances,
continuing through seeming change
and knowing all experiences.

This is the unseen, common ground
of self-illuminating light,
which knows all difference and change. *from*
It cannot change or pass away. *3.12.6-7*

It is the background of the world
outside each personality.
It is the core of mind and heart
within each personality.
It is found everywhere, complete,
continuing through everything.

Who knows this achieves fulfilment, *from*
realizes deathlessness. *3.12.7-9*

The principle of light

There is a light beyond all lights:

which lights up all reflected things,
which lights the dark of lightlessness,
which lights each shining source of light.

This light of lights and lightlessness *from*
is here within each one of us. *3.13.7*

It's seen in sight and sightlessness;
it's felt through warmth of living touch;
it's heard when hearing turns away
from outward sounds, and hears instead
the fire blazing here within.

Who heeds this light, in sight and sound
and mind and all appearances,
sees beauty shining everywhere;
hears harmony in everything;

and realizes every thought
and feeling as a seeming wave
of unconditioned, changeless truth *from*
and unaffected happiness. *3.13.8*

Reality and self [2]

In truth, this many seeming world
is only one reality,
in which all things seem to be born,
seem to live on and pass away.

For those who look, in tranquil peace,
where all appearances arise,
where all appearances are based,
and where they all dissolve again,
truth shines in all its clarity.

Each personality is made
of inclinations, good and bad.
Each person's inclinations now
build future personality.

By choosing to incline this way
or that, each one of us builds up *from*
what later on our lives will be. *3.14.1*

Through all the changes of our lives,
in every personality,
each one of us experiences
a sense of self, that each calls 'I'.

It is the knowing principle
within our minds, the principle
of life within all living things,
the principle of consciousness
that lights up all appearances.

In all conceptions it is truth:
the background of reality
in all the things we seem to see.

[2]See *Interpreting the Upanishads*, pages 23-26, for an indication of how this retelling interprets the original text.

It is the ground on which we stand,
the ground of all created things
we see or hear, conceive or feel.
It is the basis of all sense,
all thought, all sensibility.

Beyond all partial, bounded forms
by which it seems to be expressed,
beyond all troubles of the mind
and body in this seeming world, *from*
self is untroubled, always free. *3.14.2*

This self within each person's heart ...

is smaller than the smallest thing
that eyes can see or mind conceive ...

is greater than the whole wide earth
beneath our feet; is greater than
the sky's expanse above our heads,
than any far-flung universe
that instruments can show to us,
than all the complex, subtle worlds *from*
imagination can conceive. *3.14.3*

In truth, this self within each heart
is absolute reality:
found everywhere, in everything,
beyond all things that seem to be.

Where outside things have been perceived
through body's senses or through mind,
perception introduces doubt
that mind or body may be wrong.

But where the world's appearances
are left behind and self is found,
there self directly knows itself.

It knows because it is itself,
and thus no room remains for doubt.

Whoever realizes self
knows finally, beyond all doubt, *from*
unbounded, deathless certainty. *3.14.4*

Sacrifice[3]

Life in this world is sacrifice.
The years of youth are sacrificed
to morning gods of waking earth.
The years that follow youth are spent
in sacrifice to midday gods
of struggle to achieve success.
Old age is spent in sacrifice
to evening gods of glowing light, *from*
as body's powers ebb away. *3.16*

Hunger, want, unhappiness
show us the need for sacrifice.
Satisfaction, joy, success
develop courage, lessen fear.
Ethics, truth and discipline
diminish petty selfishness.
Laughter, love, vitality
reduce our sense of separateness.

Life's sacrifice begins with birth,
goes on through every seeming breath
and only ends at ego's death;
when self is truly realized
as our changeless, deathless essence: *from*
sole source of life, pure consciousness. *3.17.1-6*

Self is the ancient, timeless seed
from which all life and world are born.
Through all that seems obscurity,
self shines undimmed as consciousness,
the light that lights all other lights.

That light is self, and self alone. *from 3.17.7*

[3]See *Interpreting the Upanishads*, pages 29-30, for an indication of how part of this retelling interprets the original text (in particular 3.17.7).

Subjective and objective [4]

Subjectively, the thinking
principle may be considered
all reality, all that there is.

And then objectively, the background
of the world, continuing
through all appearances in space
and time, may be considered all
there is, all true reality.

Both of these meditations are
advised: the first subjectively, *from*
the second one objectively. *3.18.1*

[4]See *Interpreting the Upanishads*, pages 68-69, for an indication of how this retelling interprets the original text.

The self in everyone [5]

King Ashvapati Kaikeya
was once approached by a small group
of learned householders, who asked:

'Sir, we have heard that you have knowledge
of a "universal" self.
Could you explain this self to us?'

King Ashvapati, in reply,
said: 'Tell me, first, just what you think
this "universal" self might be.'

One thought this self was starry heaven,
which rules what happens in the world.

Another thought this self was sun,
illuminating world below.

A third believed this self was air,
the subtle breath of qualities.

A fourth believed this self was space,
pervading all that it contains.

A fifth believed this self was water,
flowing into changing forms.

The sixth believed this self was matter, *from*
constituting everything. *5.11-17*

King Ashvapati said to them:

'In all these different, partial views
of one same "universal" self,
you draw upon experience
as if you know this self as something
different from each one of you.

[5]See *Interpreting the Upanishads*, pages 139-141, for an indication of how this retelling interprets the original text.

'But, surely, "universal" self
is just that self which all of us
see in ourselves in different ways.

'Beneath these different points of view,
just what is it that's really here,
shared in common by us all?

'Beneath the many differences
through which our bodies, minds and senses
view the world, upon what common
measure of all measured things
do we rely, in order that
such differences may be compared?

'Our knowledge of the world is built
by joining different measurements.
But on what base? Is there in us
one common base of measurement:
to which each one of us refers
for everything that's measured here
in anyone's experience?

'This common base of measurement
is found by turning thought back in:
to knowing self, from which thought comes.
This is the self in each of us.

'It's the unmixed intensity
of thought that's known as thought alone:
where knowing self is objectless,
pure consciousness that knows all things
as nothing else but self alone.

'For one who knows this, all experience
everywhere is drawn upon:
whatever worlds may seem conceived,
whatever beings may appear, *from*
however seen by seeming selves.' *5.18.1*

Where knowledge comes from[6]

Young Shvetaketu, twelve years old,
was sent away from home to learn
what custom said that he should know.

At twenty-four, his education
seemed complete and he came back,
proud of all that he had learned.

His father said: 'But have you learned
to question what you do not know?

'And have you ever asked yourself
how you may learn what has not been
already learned, how you may think
of something that is yet unthought,
how we may know reality
beyond the bounds of seeming knowledge
that our partial minds conceive?'

'No, I have not been taught this way. *from*
I do not know quite what you mean.' *6.1.1-3*

'Consider, then, a piece of clay.
Through it the substance "clay" is known.
And thus, in knowing just this piece,
the common nature of all clay
is known, and tells of other things
that also may be made of clay.

'Through differences of name and form
in different objects made of clay,
one common substance, "clay", is known.
And thus, beneath appearances,
we recognize reality
beyond the bounds of name and form *from*
our changing minds appear to see. *6.1.4*

[6]See *Interpreting the Upanishads*, pages 27-29 and 203-204, for an indication of how parts of this retelling interpret the original text (in particular: 6.12.1-3 and 6.14.1-2, respectively).

'Some say that all created things
are only seeming names and forms
that rise from empty nothingness.

'But then, what are appearances?
If they are names, what do they name?
What is it that appears through all
the many, changing forms we see?
What is it that through different forms
is shown by these appearances?

'Appearances are nothing else
but different forms of consciousness,
which shines in every one of us
and lights up all we seem to see.

'Through seeming mind, this consciousness
appears transformed in changing shapes
that represent a varied world
of forms and names and qualities.

'But mind is partial; every shape
it forms leaves something out,
unformed, unnamed, unqualified.

'Thus forms and names and qualities
divide the world that mind perceives,
and seem to show us separate things.

'What are these separate-seeming things?
They all arise in consciousness,
continue on in consciousness,
and come to end in consciousness.

'They cannot rise, continue on
or end, apart from consciousness.
All that they are is consciousness.

'Through all appearances of mind, *from*
reality is consciousness; *6.2-4,*
for nothing else is ever known. *6.8.2-7*

'When mind dissolves in depth of sleep,
no seeming object can remain
and no reflected light is seen.
There, consciousness shines clarified,
unmixed with alien-seeming things.

'To outward sight, deep sleep may seem
a state of empty nothingness;

'but, seen itself, in its own sight,
deep sleep dissolves appearances
in self-illuminating light,
where all of being stands revealed *from*
as unconditioned consciousness. *6.8.1*

'As honey holds within itself
sweet nectars drawn from many flowers,
and as these flower-nectars, merged,
have lost all sense of separateness;

'so also consciousness contains
the essence of all sights, all sounds,
all thoughts and all appearances
that knowledge gathers from the world.

'And these appearances of world,
when taken in and understood, *from*
are merged as one in consciousness. *6.9*

'Flowing rivers are but water;
changing life is consciousness.
Mind and body change each moment;
objects seem to come and go.

'Consciousness is always present,
always here in all experience;
it is that which never leaves us,
that which each of us calls "I".

'It is not a seeming object
mind or senses can perceive.
It cannot be a partial piece
of world, confined in space or time.

'It is complete, here in each heart,
in every smallest particle
of everything we seem to see.

'And yet, all space, all time, all things, *from*
all minds are found contained in it.' *6.10*

Then, Shvetaketu's father led
him to a spreading banyan tree,
whose fruits had fallen on the ground.

'Pick up a fruit.... Break it open....
Tell me what you see.' 'Tiny seeds.'

'Break one of these.... What do you see?' *from*
'Nothing. The seeds are much too small.' *6.12.1*

'And yet, within each tiny seed,
there is a subtle something which
your eyes don't see, something unseen
from which this spreading tree has grown.

'So too, from unmixed consciousness,
which mind and senses can't perceive, *from*
arises this great-seeming world. *6.12.2*

'Pure consciousness, the essence of
each mind and heart, is all the world's
reality. That is the truth. *from*
That is what you really are.' *6.12.3*

Next, Shvetaketu's father took
some salt and gave it to his son:
'Put this in a jar of water,
leave it overnight and come back
here again tomorrow morning.'

When Shvetaketu came again
his father asked: 'Take out the salt.'

'I cannot, Sir. It has dissolved, *from*
and cannot now be seen at all.' *6.13.1*

'Then take a sip … a little sip,
just from the top.… How does it taste?'

'It's salty, Sir.' 'Now pour out half,
and sip again.… How does it taste,
now, at the middle of the jar?'

'It's salty, Sir, again.' 'Now pour
out nearly all the water, taste
the last bit at the bottom.… How
does it taste now?' 'Still salty, Sir.'

'Although you cannot see the salt,
you find it present everywhere,
throughout that water in the jar.

'So too, though consciousness itself
can never be perceived by mind
or by the senses, it is here:
self-evident in all we see, *from*
throughout this seeming universe. *6.13.2*

'Pure consciousness, the essence of
each mind and heart, is all the world's
reality. It is the truth. *from*
That is what you really are.' *6.13.3*

'How can this truth be understood?'

'Suppose a man, blindfolded, finds
himself quite lost in a strange place *from*
and wanders, crying out for help. *6.14.1*

'Suppose that someone takes away
the blindfold from his eyes, and shows
him how to seek and find his way.

'Then he can journey on, from place
to place, and get back home again.

'So too, a teacher shows you how
to seek and find your way back home
to your own self: where consciousness
is unconditioned, simple truth *from*
at one with all reality.' *6.14.2*

Learning and knowledge

Nārada, though greatly learned,
found his mind consumed by doubt.
So he asked Sanatkumāra:

'What's the use of sacred scriptures,
all these sciences and arts?
How am I to understand
the many different points of view
that learning endlessly debates?

'If I don't know quite what I am …
if I don't know quite where I stand …
if I don't know from where I see …

'how can I tell what sense to make
of all this seeming conflict and
confusion of appearances
that mind and senses bring to me?

'I've heard it said that truth of self
dispels all ignorance and doubt.
But till I know this truth, it seems
that all I learn will be just words.'

Sanatkumāra laughed, and said:
'Well if you've learned the words, then all
you have to do is understand
these words, as names which represent *from*
the knowledge that you wish to know. *7.1.1-3*

'Senses see their own sensations,
all contained in seeming mind.

'Mind perceives its own perceptions,
changing with each passing moment,
each perception passing on and
giving way to new perceptions:

'thus creating time's apparent
stream of flowing restlessness.

'But, in this stream of changing sights
and sounds, sensations, feelings, thoughts,
interpretations, intuitions;

'something makes this stream continue,
something which must carry on.

'Each name we use must represent
something perceived in different ways:
through different sights and different thoughts,
in different minds, at different times.

'And this, which each name represents,
continuing through differences
of personality and time,
is what we call "reality".

'In every object that we name,
reality remains the same
no matter how we look at it;
no matter how appearances
may seem to differ and to change,
through changes in our point of view.

'Thus, every name we use must name *from*
reality, which carries on *7.1.4*
while mind and its perceptions change. *–7.2.2*

'As mind's perceptions come and go,
each one is known by consciousness:
which lights up all appearances,
in different minds, at different times.

'This consciousness is always here,
continuing through differences
of personality and time,
through changing views, through passing time,
in everything we seem to see.

'This common, changeless consciousness
is that reality which stays
the same, in every one of us;
while our minds and bodies vary,
changing what we seem to be.

'Through all the claims that ego makes
to be a body in the world,
or a mind within the body,
consciousness is what we are.

'The self that each of us calls "I"
is nothing else but consciousness.

'In all experience, consciousness
is that which knows appearances;
reality is that which stays
the same, while changing views give rise
to different appearances.

'Reality and consciousness
are never separate; both are there
throughout experience; neither can
be known apart. In truth, they are
but different names for one same thing.

'Reality is nothing else
but consciousness, the real self *from*
that each of us calls "I".' *7.3-15*

Though this made sense to Nārada,
his mind again conceived a doubt:

'How may such knowledge be applied,
in practice, to a person's life;
when truth is known but mind returns
to face the seeming world again?'

'Where truth is rightly understood,
it shines expressed in words and acts.

'Unsought, unplanned by act of will,
it rises up spontaneously
and shines directly from within; *from*
because its nature is to shine. *7.16-21*

'What do we seek in all our acts?

'All that we seek is happiness;
and happiness is found where self
no longer seems at odds with world,

'where separate-seeming self dissolves *from*
in fullness of reality. *7.22*

'All misery and want arise
from incomplete experience,
where self seems somehow incomplete *from*
for want of something it desires. *7.23*

'But where reality and self
are realized as only one;
there incompleteness can't arise, *from*
nor misery, nor want, nor death. *7.24*

'Where it's believed that alien objects
are perceived, desired or known;
there it must seem that self is ego,
caught up in its limitations,
hurt by pain, afraid of dying, *from*
born to live in pettiness. *7.25*

'But where the truth is understood
that nothing else is seen or heard
or thought or felt but self alone;
there all ego is transcended,
unmixed joy is realized.

'When truth is effortlessly known
in every sight and every sound, in each
perception, thought and feeling; *from*
knowledge then has been applied.' *7.26*

Change and self [7]

Our bodies, senses and our minds
keep changing in a changing world.
And so, whatever they perceive
is by its nature changeable.

But, as this change keeps going on,
how is it known that things have changed?
How can something be compared
with what it was before it changed?

Where variation is perceived,
what is it that knows the change
of passing states which come and go?

It must be there before the change,
to know the state that was before.
And it must still be there when change
has taken place, to know what has
become of what was there before.

Wherever there is variation,
that which knows must carry on
through changing states that come and go.

Each state gives way to other states,
but that which knows the change remains.

This knowing principle remains
unchanged, unvarying: through all
the change and all the variations
body, sense and mind perceive.

Whatever is perceived must vary;
that which knows is never changed.

[7]See *Interpreting the Upanishads*, pages 76-81 and 167-170, for an indication of how parts of this retelling interpret the original text (in particular: 8.1.1,3-5 together with 8.4.1-2; and 8.1.5-6 together with 8.2.10 and 8.3.1-2; respectively).

As body, sense and mind perceive,
appearances of world are formed.
And all of these appearances
are known by light of consciousness.

Perception isn't that which knows;
it only forms appearances
through changing body, sense and mind.

That which knows is consciousness;
it lights up all appearances.
It's always there, throughout experience,
always shines by its own light.

Perception changes every moment;
consciousness remains unchanged.

At the surface of our minds,
things appear and disappear:
as attention is directed
from one object to the next.

Beneath this stream of changing show,
different things must be related
at the background of experience,
where each thing is understood.

As mind's outer surface changes,
consciousness continues on,
putting different things together
at the depth of understanding:
changeless background of experience, *from*
inner basis of the mind. *8.1.1*

This unchanging consciousness,
which shines within each mind and heart,
has neither magnitude nor form.

And yet, we find contained in it
everything we seem to see:
all the entire universe
of earth and sun and moon and stars, *from*
all space, all time, all worlds, all minds. *8.1.3*

If all existence is thus found
within each person's mind and heart,
what happens when a person dies?

Can all of being be destroyed,
when some poor mind in little body *from*
suffers harm and passes on? *8.1.4*

In truth, as mind and body seem
to suffer harm and die, such harm
and death are mere appearances,
which cannot rise or stand except
as they are known by consciousness.

But consciousness illuminates
itself; it shines by its own light.
It does not rise or pass away.

It is the self, within us all,
whose nature is to light itself,
and thus to light appearances
which are themselves but consciousness.

True self, as unmixed consciousness,
depends on nothing else at all.
It is untouched by seeming change *from*
or seeming harm or seeming death. *8.1.5*

Ego claiming to be body
lives in bondage to the world.
Ego claiming to be mind
lives in bondage to desire.
All that mind and body do
gets undone in course of time.

When an object is desired,
ego feels that self is lacking
something to be found outside.
Consciousness thus seems divided;
mind appears, dissatisfied.

When an object of desire
is attained; then, for the moment,
restless ego has subsided,
self seems to have been completed,
consciousness seems unified.

Thus, truth of self, within the heart,
shines out as peace and happiness. *from 8.1.5-6 and 8.2*

But though achievement of desire
brings a state of happiness,
such happiness can never last;

for ego rises up again,
inherently dissatisfied,
and seeks some further alien thing.

All of ego's life and actions
are dependent on the self;
which, through seeming self-deception,
ego does not understand. *from 8.3.1*

Self is thus a buried treasure
ego keeps on walking over,
vainly feeling needs and wants
for things that seem outside itself.

Always seeking alien objects,
ego does not understand
that the goal of all desire
is true self, within the heart;
for all reality is here. *from 8.3.2*

Self is the continuity
that lives unchanged through change; it is
the bridge that joins all differences.

And yet, it also is the basis
of discrimination, by which
different things are told apart.

When understanding passes from
appearance to reality,
no day or night, no height or depth,
no age, nor death, nor fear, nor grief,
nor good or bad can pass to self;

for no conditioned quality *from*
of seeming world applies to it. *8.4.1*

As truth of self is realized,
all blindness is removed from sight,
all wounds are healed, all pain dissolves,
all bonds are loosed, all lack is filled;

and darkness shines as dazzling light *from*
of unconditioned consciousness. *8.4.2*

In search of self[8]

'The real self, in each of us,
is stainless, undecaying,
free from hunger, free from thirst,
untroubled in the midst of grief.

'It has no thought nor wish, but truth.
This is the self we cannot help but seek,
the truth we seek to understand.

'Whoever sees and knows this self
gains all the world, and finds
the goal of all desires.'

These words, the gods and demons heard,
were said by Lord Prajāpati,
the Lord of all created things.

To seek this self that gains the world
and finds the goal of all desire,
the gods and demons sent their chiefs
to question him that made the world.

Thus Indra, chief among the gods,
and demon-king Virocana
left home and came, in search of truth,
before their Lord Prajāpati.

Each came with fuel grasped in hand,
to show their wish that ignorance *from*
should burn in sacrificial flame. *8.7.1-2*

They put aside their finery,
their shining ornaments and crowns,
their life of outward wealth and power.

Thirty-two years they lived instead
the humble life of supplicants,
who would prepare themselves to learn.

[8]See *Interpreting the Upanishads*, pages 123-139, for an indication of how this retelling interprets the original text.

Until at last Prajāpati
asked: 'What is it you wish to know?'

They said: 'We've heard that you describe
a stainless, undecaying self
by which desires are attained. *from*
This self is what we wish to find.' *8.7.3*

'Then what you seek is close at hand,'
was the reply. 'For self is seen
where sight looks back into itself.
It is the changeless absolute,
where death and fear do not arise.'

'But Sir,' they asked, 'what is it that
a person sees reflected in
the stillness of a shining pool *from*
or in a mirror's clarity?' *8.7.4*

'See for yourselves,' was the reply.
'One same reality is seen
in everything. Go look into
a pool of water, and then say
what you may find reflected there.'

Thus, Indra and Virocana
went to a nearby pool and looked
and said: 'We see of course ourselves, *from*
down to our hair and fingernails.' *8.8.1*

Prajāpati then said to them:

'Now dress in all your finery,
put on your crowns and ornaments;
then look again into the pool *from*
and say what is reflected there.' *8.8.2*

They dressed and looked and said with pride:
'We see ourselves as we should be,
dressed as befits our kingly state.'

Prajāpati's reply was brief:

'Whatever you may think you see,
all that you see is only self.
It is complete reality,
where death and fear do not arise.'

Then satisfaction seemed to dawn
on Indra and Virocana.
It seemed that there was nothing left
to learn; and so they took their leave *from*
and made their way towards their homes. *8.8.3*

But, as they left, Prajāpati
looked sadly after them and thought:

'They haven't understood at all.
Their faith clings on to false beliefs.
Whoever lives by such belief
stays caught in futile misery.'

Virocana, triumphantly,
went back into his demon world,
where he proclaimed: 'Our selves come first!

'Let us be strong, increase our power,
and take by force what we desire.
Let's feed and clothe and arm ourselves,
to satisfy our needs and build
our strength to do just as we please.

'For it befits our demon state
that world be bent to serve our needs *from*
and wishes, as embodied selves.' *8.8.4*

But Indra, on his way back home,
was troubled by a nagging doubt:

'If self is body, it enjoys
good fortune as the body does.

'When body is well-dressed ... so too
is self; when body gains in wealth
and power and grace ... so too does self.

'But, when the body's eyes are dimmed,
when body's wealth and power fade,
when grace departs; then it would seem …

'that self, like body, must decay,
that self, like body, suffers loss
of sight and wealth and power and grace.

'I *can't* be satisfied with this.' *from 8.9.1*

Thus Indra turned and went again
before his Lord Prajāpati,
again with fuel grasped in hand
to show his unburned ignorance.

'What brings you back? You seemed so pleased
when, just a little while ago,
you left with King Virocana.'

Indra explained his troubled doubt,
and lived for thirty-two more years
a student's dedicated life;

until Prajāpati spoke out
again, in different words, about
the truth that Indra wished to learn: *from 8.9.2-3*

> 'Where body's world
> dissolves in dream
> and mind is free,
> the self shines there.
>
> 'It is the deathless,
> fearless absolute.'

And now to Indra, once again,
it seemed that he had understood.

He took his leave and started out
towards his home. But on his way
a further doubt disturbed his mind
and brought him back to learn some more;

again with fuel in his hand,
by which he showed his wish to burn
the ignorance that still remained.

Prajāpati asked: 'What is it
that brings you back again so soon?'

Indra explained: 'The self in dream
may not be bound to suffer those
same ills that trouble body in
the waking world of outer things.

'When outward eyes no longer see
and body has thus lost its sight,
the self in dreams still seems to see.
And when gross, outward body dies,
perhaps the self lives on in dream.

'But, even in the state of dreams,
the self does not seem fully free.
In many dreams, self seems to fear,
seems to be driven, hunted down;
it seems in pain, it seems to weep,
it seems to suffer death and grief.

'I *can't* be satisfied with this.'

So Indra stayed for thirty-two
more years again; and when this time
had passed away, Prajāpati *from*
spoke out these words that he might learn: *8.10.1-4*

> 'In depth of sleep
> which knows no dream,
> self shines as peace.
>
> 'It is the fearless,
> deathless absolute.'

Yet once again, it seemed that truth
had dawned in Indra's searching mind.
But yet again, returning home,
poor Indra's mind was seized by doubt.

And yet again, his wish to burn
the ignorance that still remained
was shown by fuel in his hand;
as he returned, in search of truth,
before his Lord Prajāpati.

He told his doubt: 'The sleeping self
can't know itself by any thought
that "I am this" or "I am that" ...

'Nor does it know any object
other than itself; and, therefore,
it seems quite annihilated ...

'In depth of sleep, there seems to be
no self at all. Does this mean self
is blank or empty nothingness?
How can this be? There's something here *from*
I don't quite rightly understand.' *8.11.1-2*

Prajāpati said: 'If you wait
another five years here, I shall
explain again; though really there
is nothing further to explain.'

So Indra lived there five years more;
thus making it a total of
one hundred and one years he lived
a student's life, instructed by
his teacher, Lord Prajāpati.

When the time came, Prajāpati *from*
enlightened Indra with these words: *8.11.3*

> 'This body is mortal;
> it belongs to death.
> But in it lives
> the deathless self,
> which has no body.

'Wherever life
is mixed with body,
like is followed
by dislike,
pleasure alternates
with pain.

'Whoever mixes
life with body
seeks escape
in passing pleasures,
can't escape
from feeling pain.

'The real self
transcends the body,
has no need for
passing pleasures,
is untouched *from*
by body's pain. *8.12.1*

'When morning wisps
of mist and cloud
rise up towards
the peace and
clarity of sky,

'they shine revealed
as bodiless,
dissolving radiant *from*
into light. *8.12.2*

'So too, when forms
of seeming mind
approach the peace
of dreamless sleep,

'they are dissolved
in unobscured,
untroubled clarity;

'revealing self
for what it is:

'pure, bodiless
unfading light
of unconditioned
consciousness.

'This is the real self,
remaining always free:

'untroubled by the body
where we falsely think
self has been born,

'and where self seems
to laugh, eat, play,
to seek out pleasure,
love and happiness.

'But where the self
is thought to be
encumbered by
the body's needs,

'there life seems caught
in bondage:
like a horse
that's tethered *from*
to a cart. *8.12.3*

'The eye is just
an instrument
for seeing sights.

'The ear is just
an instrument
for hearing sounds.

'The voice is just
an instrument
for speaking words.

'The mind is just
an instrument
for thinking thoughts

'and dreaming up
a subtle world
from feeling and desire.

'But, in each one of us,
it is the self that knows

'the sights that seeing sees,
the sounds that hearing hears,
the words that speaking speaks,

'the thoughts that thinking thinks,
and all the subtle worlds
that dreaming dreams *from*
from feeling and desire. *8.12.4-5*

'This knowing self,
this common core
of unconditioned consciousness
within each personality,

'is that immortal absolute
to which the gods pay heed,
by which they gain their power.

'This very self,
within us all,
is what we seek
in all of our desires.

'Whoever sees and knows this self
gains all the world, and finds *from*
the goal of all desire.' *8.12.6*

From the Kena Upanishad

The unmoved mover [1]

What motivates mind's changing show
of seeming objects, thoughts, desires?

What makes the mind go out to things
that seem to be outside itself?

What sends the mind, in soaring flight,
to search for freedom, happiness?

From what does mind come down again,
to earth: where joy seems always bound
to pettiness and suffering?

What joins together various acts –
of body, sense and mind – to make
each person's individual life?

From what does meaning come: into
the things we do, the words we speak,
the gestures that our bodies make?

What common light co-ordinates
our differing perceptions *from*
into fuller knowledge of the world? *1.1*

One common, inner principle
of consciousness is found in life,
in mind and senses, words and acts.

[1]See *Interpreting the Upanishads*, pages 115-118, for an indication of how part of this retelling interprets the original text (in particular 1.1-9).

Those who are brave break free from world's
appearances, and realize
that self is unmixed consciousness: *from*
beyond all seeming change and death. *1.2*

This truth cannot be reached by mind
or senses, nor described by speech.

Nor can such faculties explain *from*
the way in which it may be taught. *1.3*

In truth, the self, as consciousness,
is not an object that is known;
nor is it anything unknown.

Its knowledge comes from ancient times.
Its knowledge comes before all time;
for it must first be known before *from*
the very thought of time can rise. *1.4*

It isn't something conjured up
by words and thoughts; instead, it is
the ever-present, knowing ground:

from which all thoughts and words arise,
on which all thoughts and words depend, *from*
to which all thoughts and words return. *1.5*

It isn't something thought by mind;
instead, it is the principle
of consciousness that lights the mind: *from*
by which all mind and thoughts are known. *1.6*

It isn't something seen by sight,
or heard by listening; instead,
it is the knowing principle *from*
that lights all sight and sound and sense. *1.7-8*

It isn't something breathed by breath
or lived by life; instead, it is
the living principle by which
all breath and life are vitalized.

This knowing principle of life
is not a partial object, not
some little part of world, to which
our minds and senses can attend.

Instead, it is the common ground
of all appearances that show
some part of world, perceived
by partial body, sense and mind.

This common ground is all there is.
It is complete reality,
which each appearance shows in part.

It's known in full as knowing self:
as pure, unchanging consciousness *from*
beneath all personality. *1.9*

Wherever mind thinks that it knows,
there truth itself cannot be known;
but only partial forms appear,
of personality and world.

Such partial forms mix truth
with ignorance and falsity,
thus distorting what they show
and telling little that is true.

The question here to ask is what *from*
is meant, when someone says: 'I know.' *2.1*

Just what is it in us that knows?

It isn't really mind, for all
mind does is form appearances
before the light of consciousness.

It's only consciousness that knows:
by lighting mind's perceptions, thoughts
and feelings, as they come and go.

It's only consciousness that is *from*
the 'I' which knows experience. *2.2*

Where mind presumes to know, it lies.

If 'I' is claimed to be the mind,
the thought 'I know' is treacherous;
for then it must be compromised
by also thinking 'I don't know',
to mitigate mind's ignorance.

Pure consciousness, the real 'I',
is that which knows, and only knows:

it knows when mind appears to know
and thus it lights all seeming things;

it knows when mind seems not to know
and thus it shows mind's ignorance.

To think of it, mind must reflect
back to the source from which thought comes,
on which mind stands as thought appears,
and where all thought returns, dissolved.

Where any thought of it remains,
it cannot there be understood.

It can't be learned by learned forms; *from*
it's learned where learning is unlearned. *2.3*

Through every changing state of mind
consciousness continues on,
the changeless base of seeming change,
untouched itself by change and death.

When mind turns in towards the self,
the source of every strength is found;
and self is known as consciousness, *from*
life's deathless, unconditioned ground. *2.4*

If changeless consciousness is seen
here in the world of seeming things,
truth shines as peace and happiness.

If consciousness becomes obscured,
unhappiness and loss result.

By seeing through appearances
and finding truth in everything, *from*
deathlessness is realized. *2.5*

Desire's end [2]

Objectively, seen from the world
created by our faculties
of outward sense, truth seems to shine
only in blinding flashes of
divine illumination that
immediately dissolve all sense
of the created universe, *from*
thus passing on from changing time. *4.4*

Subjectively, seen where the mind
turns back to self from which it comes,
truth is at once both goal and base.

It's that to which all mind aspires,
and that on which all mind depends:

as it appears to carry on
through changing time, enabling world
to be conceived by seeming mind *from*
from fragments of past memory. *4.5*

Truth is just that which is desired
beneath all seeming goals of mind.

It's that which all desire seeks,
and it should thus be understood:
beneath the many different forms
imagined by our partial minds
to represent the truth they seek.

Whoever knows this truth of love *from*
is loved, in truth, by everyone. *4.6*

[2]See *Interpreting the Upanishads*, pages 162-164, for an indication of how this retelling interprets the original text.

From the Kaushītaki Upanishad

For and against [1]

For knowledge that agrees, I am.
For knowing contrary, I am.

I am the knowing principle
that's common to all different views
and carries on through changing time:

as differing perceptions join
in unity of single truth;
as differences are told apart,
thus knowing truth from falsity. *from 1.2*

[1]This retelling is an interpretation of the following short passage that occurs towards the end of 1.2.

... samtad-vide'ham	For knowing together with that, I am.
pratitad-vide'ham ...	For knowing contrary to that, I am.

Each being's self

I'm here: in every passing season,
in the cycling of the seasons
risen from their background source,
continuing through space and time.

I am the seed of consciousness
that's always here in all experience:

lighting every passing moment,
common to all different moments,
changeless through all changing time.

I am each being's real self,
the truth of all reality.

This truth is *immanent* in all
that is perceived: as that which *is*,
unmixed with mere appearances
attributed by sense and mind.

This truth also *transcends* whatever
is perceived: as that which *knows*,
as unconditioned consciousness,
the common, knowing principle
from which all sense and mind arise.

Thus seen *'out there'* and found *'in here'*,
truth is complete reality: *from*
known everywhere, in everything. *1.6*

The basis of mind

'Just what enables thoughts, desires,
and the objects that they seek?'

'It's nothing else but consciousness:
pure, unconditioned consciousness, *from*
unmixed with any alien thing.' *1.7*

The living principle

The living principle in each
of us is all reality.

Mind is its intermediary
towards our outward faculties:
expression is its instrument
of outward action in the world;
perception is its outward watch;
attention makes its presence known.

To find it, one must turn perception
back from outward-going acts,
to ask instead what acts express.

Behind all actions in the world
are the perceptions they express.

Behind perceptions of the world
is the attention of the mind,
which turns from one thing to the next.

Behind the changing mind is this
one living principle of truth:

one unconditioned consciousness,
which stays the same while mind is changed
from one appearance to the next.

This changeless principle of truth
is always here, in each of us.
It is the centre of all life,
from which all seeming faculties
of body, sense and mind arise.

It has no needs, makes no demands;
it never suffers want or lack;
it does not ask for anything.

And yet, spontaneously, unasked,
all that is done is done for it.

To this sole centre of all life,
all faculties bring offering.
To this complete reality
all actions finally return;
and here they give themselves to peace,
dissolved at last in what they seek.

Where truth is found, all questions end
and there is nothing left to ask.

All comes unasked, spontaneously, *from*
where truth has finally been found. *2.1-2*

Continuing truth

When speech comes to an end, what then
becomes of truth that has been told?

As speech dies off, perceptions rise,
expressing truth that has been told;
and truth is thus continued on....

But when perceptions end, what then
becomes of truth that was perceived?

Perceptions die, but thoughts arise,
expressing truth that was perceived;
and truth is thus continued on....

Then in their turn, when thoughts pass on,
where is the truth they thought about?

As thoughts die off, emotions rise,
expressing truth to which thought led;
and truth is thus continued on....

But when emotions end, what then
becomes of truth that has been felt?

When feelings die, they are absorbed
into that background consciousness
which carries on through seeming change:
as different feelings, thoughts, perceptions
come and go in changing mind.

This is the background of all life,
the changeless, living principle
of underlying consciousness:

in which perceptions, thoughts and feelings
are absorbed; from which new feelings,
thoughts and actions are expressed.

And in this living principle
of unconditioned consciousness
which is each person's real self,
truth always carries on unchanged: *from*
beyond all seeming time and death. *2.13-14*

The knowing self [2]

I am the living principle
of consciousness, the real self:

the subtle spirit of all life,
the spirit of each living breath,
expressed in every living act.

This principle is life itself,
beneath all thought of seeming death.
Where it is found, there is no death.

Wherever it is seen in body,
changing body seems to live.
But where it's seen to leave the body,
body seems to die away.

It's that which makes the body's
actions seem to be alive: expressing
order, purpose, thought and feeling,
thus expressing consciousness.

Approaching it as life itself,
it's understood as deathlessness.

Approaching it as consciousness,
it's known as unconditioned truth.

By knowing self as deathless life,
the essence of all life is reached,
unchanged through seeming change and death.

Each living personality
seems made of different faculties:
each one expressing consciousness
in its own ways, at its own times.

And yet these different faculties
somehow express a unity
of knowledge that co-ordinates

[2] See *Interpreting the Upanishads*, pages 91-94, for an indication of how parts of this retelling interpret the original text (in particular 3.2-3).

names that are known by speaking them,
sights that are known by seeing them,
sounds that are known by hearing them,
thoughts that are known by thinking them.

As different objects are thus known
in different ways, at different times,
through different seeming faculties,

these different ways of knowing things
reflect a unifying base
of underlying consciousness
on which each faculty depends.

Thus when speech speaks, all other
faculties are somehow understood
to be expressed in what is said.

Or when sight sees, all other
faculties are somehow understood
to be expressed in what is seen.

When hearing hears, all other
faculties are somehow understood
to be expressed in what is heard.

And when mind thinks, all other
faculties are somehow understood
to be expressed in what is thought.

Within these living faculties,
one common principle of life
is shared beneath their differences.

And this one living principle, *from*
though from within, contains them all. *3.2*

What is essential to all life?

It cannot be the faculty
of speech; for there are those whom we
call 'dumb', who do not speak, but who
are still essentially alive.

Nor can it be the faculties
of sight or hearing; for we know
of those whom we call 'blind' or 'deaf',
who do not see or do not hear,
but who are still essentially alive.

And further too, we know of those
whose loss of outward sight or hearing
even strengthens inner life.

Nor can life's essence be the mind.
For can we say that life has gone,
where understanding is attained
and all mind's complex, changing acts
come to an end in simple truth?

Or can we say that life is missing,
where desires are achieved
and mind dissolves in happiness?

And can we say that life is absent
in the state of dreamless sleep,
where mind's perceptions, thoughts and feelings
all dissolve in rest and peace?

Life is essentially the source
from which all living acts arise.
It is the ground on which they stand,
and into which they are absorbed
when they return to source again.

Thus truly known, life in itself
is consciousness, the real self:
which holds this body all around
and causes it to rise, alive.

Wherever life is seen in body,
consciousness is found implied.

Wherever consciousness is seen
expressed in body, so is life.

Thus 'life' and 'consciousness' are
different names for one same principle:
which makes this body seem alive,
and knows all that is ever known
in everyone's experience.

As a sick person comes to death
all faculties of life dissolve.
Thus speech and hearing, sight and mind
no longer are attributed
to body when it dies away.

What happens to that person then?
What happens when perceptions, thoughts
and feelings pass away at death?

As when a person falls asleep,
so too at passing body's death,
all different-seeming faculties
of life return to unity
of unconditioned consciousness:

the underlying source of life *from*
from which all lives and minds arise. *3.3*

Each name is just an act of speaking,
which once spoken comes to end
and is absorbed in consciousness,
the underlying source from where
all speaking and all names arise.

Each sight is just an act of seeing,
which once seen comes to an end
and is absorbed in consciousness,
the underlying source from where
all seeing and all sights arise.

Each sound is just an act of hearing,
which once heard comes to an end
and is absorbed in consciousness,
the underlying source from where
all hearing and all sounds arise.

Each perception is an act
which once enacted comes to end
and is absorbed in consciousness,
the underlying source from where
all senses and perceptions rise.

Each thought is just an act of thinking,
which once thought comes to an end
and is absorbed in consciousness,
the underlying source from where
all minds and all their thoughts arise.

Here, at this underlying source
of unconditioned consciousness
that's common to all different acts,
no change or difference can apply.

All beings here are always one,
beneath their seeming differences *from*
of changing body, sense and mind. *3.4*

How then do differences appear?

They're shown by various faculties,
each of which starts from consciousness
and acts towards divided objects
of experience in the world.

Our various partial faculties
thus radiate from consciousness
to different parts of our experience,
in a world that seems to be
made up from many different things.

Our faculties of speech go out
from consciousness: to say the names
by which the world is then described.

Our faculties of choice arise
from consciousness: to pick out things
on which attention focuses.

Our faculties of sight go out
from inner light of consciousness:
to see appearances of world
and objects thus made manifest.

Our faculties of hearing rise
from consciousness: to hear the sounds
whose meaning tells what world may be.

Our faculties of taste go out
from underlying consciousness:
to taste the flavours of experience
and to judge the qualities
of objects that are thus perceived.

Our faculties of management
arise from knowing consciousness:
to manage work towards the goals
that our intentions have prescribed.

Our faculties of body rise
from consciousness: to serve the needs
of seeking comfort, lessening pain.

Creative faculties emerge
from underlying consciousness:
expressing value and enjoyment,
thus creating useful things.

Our faculties of movement rise
from this same base of consciousness:
to take our bodies and our minds,
impelled by wish, from place to place.

Our faculties of mind arise
from this same common, knowing base
of unconditioned consciousness:
to think ideas and feel desires,
conceiving world and wishing change.

Thus every living faculty
has its objective counterpart: *from*
of objects that it acts towards. *3.5*

Since every object in experience
rises through some faculty
that rises up from consciousness,
each object and each faculty
depends on knowing consciousness.

From consciousness expressed in speech,
all speaking and all names arise,
describing what has been perceived.

From consciousness expressed in choice,
all choosing by our partial minds
and all their chosen objects rise.

From consciousness expressed in sight,
all seeing and all sights arise,
and thus all seen appearances.

From consciousness expressed in hearing
and in our conceiving minds,
arise all sounds and all the meaning
that our minds conceive in them.

From consciousness expressed in taste
and in our sensibilities,
arise all flavours, qualities,
and all the values judged in them.

From consciousness expressed in work,
arise all working and all goals
that are intended by our minds.

From consciousness expressed in body,
comes all need for body's comfort
and for lessening body's pain.

From consciousness creatively
expressed, come entertainments and
designs and what we thus create.

From consciousness expressed in movement
of our bodies and our minds,
arise all movements we experience
through these bodies and these minds.

From consciousness expressed in mind,
all feelings, thoughts, perceptions rise
and hence all the apparent world *from*
that anyone experiences. *3.6*

Without the light of consciousness,
no name could be made known by speech.

Thus body's voice may speak a name,
or body's ears may hear a name,
of which one honestly could say:

'My mind was elsewhere at the time.
I was not conscious of that name.'

Without the light of consciousness,
no object of attention could
be picked by choice and focused on;

appearance could not be made known
by any faculty of sight;
no sound could be made known by hearing;
taste could not make flavour known.

Without the light of consciousness,
no management could make work known;
no body could make comfort known,
nor any needs, nor any pain;

creative acts could not make known
what they imagine or design,
nor anything that they create.

Without the light of consciousness,
no kind of movement could be known;
and no perceptions, thoughts or feelings
could arise in seeming mind.

Unlit by knowing consciousness,
no object could appear at all.

If later told some object had
been present to one's faculties,
one could in truth reply: 'My mind
was elsewhere at the time. That object
just did not appear to me.'

Without the light of consciousness,
no mind or world could be conceived.

Not even absence could be known.
One could not know one's ignorance, *from*
or know of something to be known. *3.7*

Impartial truth cannot be found
by seeking partial faculties
or partial objects in the world.

It's found by knowing that which knows.

It isn't speech one needs to know,
but that which is expressed by speech:
the knowing self that lives in speech.

It isn't choice one needs to know,
but for whose sake the choice is made:
the self that motivates the choice.

It isn't sight one needs to know,
but just the seeing principle:
which lights all seeing from within.

It isn't sound one needs to know,
but just the hearing principle:
which knows the meaning of all sound.

It isn't taste one needs to know,
but just the tasting principle:
which discerns good taste from bad.

It's not the act one needs to know,
but who is there beneath the act:
the changeless self that carries on
through different acts and knows them all,
the self for whom the acts are done.

It isn't body's pain or comfort
that one really needs to know,
but the knowing self within:
unchanged by what it knows of body,
or of comfort or of pain.

It isn't value or enjoyment
or creation one should know,
but just the living source of value:
motivating all enjoyment
in creation's changing shapes.

It isn't movement one should know,
but just the moving principle:
unmoved within all moving things,
itself entirely unchanged
yet causing all apparent change.

It isn't mind one needs to know,
but just the thinking principle:
the knowing subject of all mind.

In this subjective principle,
here at the centre of all life,
there's no diversity at all.

It's like the centre of a wheel
whose outer rim is fixed on spokes.
The spokes are fixed upon the hub,
right at the centre of the wheel.

Here, where the spokes are joined in one,
there's no diversity, nor motion
as the spokes and rim turn round.

So too, the objects of the world
are fixed on various faculties
that radiate from knowing self,
in everyone's experience.

Here, at the centre of each life,
where all our faculties are joined,
there are no different, changing things.

There's just one living principle
of unconditioned consciousness,
which is each person's real self.

It is the happiness we seek.
It does not change. It does not die.

It's not improved by doing good.
It is not harmed by any ill.
It is the changeless, uncaused cause
of all our actions in the world.

All that is done, both good and bad,
is done for it, in search of it.

It is the final principle
that rules the outer universe
and guides each person from within.

It can be known by asking on,
until no trace of doubt remains:

'What can I truly call "my self"? *from*
What is it that I really am?' *3.8*

Deep sleep and waking[3]

In depth of sleep, no mind appears
conceiving different seeming things;

and mind's attention does not direct
living energy from consciousness
to different seeming objects
in some world that mind conceives.

Thus here, in dreamless sleep, all
outward-seeming energies of life
have been withdrawn, and differences
are all dissolved in consciousness:
which shines alone, by its own light,
unmixed with any seeming thing.

Here, every day, unnoticed in
the simple peace of dreamless sleep,
all life attains to unity
of underlying consciousness,
from which all lives and minds arise.

Whenever someone falls asleep,
attention is drawn in: from world
of waking sense, through dreaming mind,
to unconditioned consciousness,
which shines unmixed in depth of sleep.

All speech, all words and all they mean,
all seeing, hearing, sights and sounds,
and all perceptions, thoughts and feelings
then dissolve: absorbed again
into their underlying base
of consciousness, from which they rise.

[3]See *Interpreting the Upanishads*, pages 48-51, for an indication of how this retelling interprets the original text.

But, when a person wakes from sleep,
outgoing energies of life
appear, through various faculties
of mind and personality.

As sparks come forth from blazing fire,
so too from consciousness come forth
the various energies of life
that mind and personality
disperse through their activities.

From these activities arise
appearances of mind and sense;
and thus, from these appearances,
the worlds that we perceive are born.

Beneath appearances of world
perceived by senses and by mind,
consciousness continues on
through every moment of experience:

lighting all appearances
that rise in dream or waking state;

and shining self-illuminated,
on its own, in depth of sleep.

It is each person's real self:
the inner principle of life
that is expressed in every act
of mind and body in the world.

All seeming selves, of body or
of sense or mind, depend upon
this real self of consciousness.

Just as a chief is represented
by his followers, who act
with his support and for his sake;

so too, the real self is
represented by the seeming selves
of body, sense and mind: whose actions
all depend on its support
and are, unknowingly or
knowingly, done only for its sake.

On consciousness, the real self,
these seeming selves always depend
for all they do or seek to do.

But it does not depend on them;
for it is there in depth of sleep,
when seeming selves have all dissolved.

As long as this true self is not
correctly understood and known,
a person's actions are not firmly
anchored in the changeless ground
from which they come, on which they stand
and where they find all that they seek.

Thus, if this ground of self remains
unknown, poor body, sense and mind
keep being overcome by their
own demons of uncertainty
and partiality and ill.

But one who knows the truth of self
has reached that certain, deathless ground
of unconditioned consciousness:

where ills have all been overcome
and freedom has, at last, been won.

from 4.19(end) and 4.20

From the Īsha Upanishad

Centre and source [1]

All this entire universe
belongs to God: who lives in it,
in every smallest bit of it.

Thus giving up all things to God,
whatever changes in this changing
universe may be enjoyed:

untainted by possessiveness,
uncompromised by wanting it.

Whatever there may be to claim, *from*
to whom, in truth, does it belong? *1*

As mind and body act in world,
a person seems to lead a life
that starts with birth and ends in death.

No other way appears than this, *from*
where life seems bound to finite acts. *2*

From blind obscurity of death
rise fearful, demon-haunted worlds,
wherever self seems to be killed.

But self, in truth, is life itself. *from*
How then can death pertain to it? *3*

It is unmoving unity;
yet mind and sense cannot catch up
with it. They always lag behind.

[1]See *Interpreting the Upanishads*, pages 180-185, for an indication of how part of this retelling interprets the original text (in particular 1, 4-8).

It is the unchanged base of change,
still centre of all happiness
which every action seeks to reach.
And yet, it always stays ahead.

Just by its nature, as it is,
unmoved itself by any act,
it is the source of energy *from*
from which all seeming actions rise. *4*

It does not move; yet it alone
is all that every movement is,
and it is all those many things
that we perceive to move and change.

To sense and mind, it's far beyond
the furthest distances of space,
much prior to the early past,
more final than the end of time.
Yet nothing else can be so close.

It's here and now: in every sight,
in every sound and smell and taste,
in every touch, in every thought
and feeling, in each mind and heart.

It is the only thing that's known
immediately; because it is
the living centre of each heart:
the knowing self we each call 'I'.

This knowing self is consciousness:
the background of appearances
that are perceived by sense and mind.

It stays through all experience,
as seeming objects come and go.

It is beyond all seeming things,
beyond the changing universe
that mind and senses seem to see.
And yet, it can be found within
each object in this seeming world.

Each seeming object that we know
is known combined with consciousness;
and thus combined with consciousness
is but a part of consciousness.

In truth, each object that we know
is nothing else but consciousness.

Though mind and sense seem to perceive
external objects in the world,
the self, in truth, knows everything
as nothing else but consciousness.

Thus, in each object, what we call
'reality' is consciousness:
which is the nature of the self.

As mind and sense see seeming things,
the self, in truth, knows but itself.

And that is plain reality:
which is beyond all seeming things; *from*
yet always *is*, in every thing. *5*

False ego is a seeming self:
a self that seems conditioned as
a little mind or body, which
is part of a much larger world.

Beneath this false identity,
of self with body or with mind,
the real self is utterly
impersonal; it is the base
of consciousness, upon which all
conditions are compared and known.

It is the unconditioned base
of all conditions in the world.

Where outward-seeming consciousness
is turned back in, towards its source,
it is dissolved in truth of self,
which is complete reality.

For everything is known in self,
and self is known in everything.

When this plain truth is realized,
what is there then to be renounced? *from*
How can disharmony arise? *6*

Where knowing is identity
of knowing self with what is known,
there known and knower are but one;

with nothing alien in between
that could obscure plain simple truth:
thus making knowledge incomplete,
creating partiality,
distorted views and nagging doubt.

For self, to know is just to be.
Its very being is to shine.

Its nature is to light itself,
without an intervening act
that could divide it from itself
or could obscure its clarity.

What grief, delusion can exist
for one who knows true unity, *from*
where everything is one with self? *7*

True self is pure, unbodied light
of unconditioned consciousness,
pervading all experience.

It has no organs, nor does it
take part in any kind of act.
No function can pertain to it.

Untouched by any harm or ill,
unstained by misery and wrong,
it is the living principle
which lights perception, knows all thought
and shines expressed as what we seek
through all our feelings and desires.

Self-evident, beyond all things
that may appear or disappear,
it simply *is*, in its own right:
completely known, beyond all doubt,
as self-illuminating light.

Upon this changeless, certain base,
each seeming thing pursues a course
of seeming change through passing time *from*
that can't be known with certainty. *8*

Unconsciousness seems blind and dark;
apparent knowledge can deceive. *from*
Yet each of these has its own use. *9-10*

Unconsciousness of passing things
can lead away from change and death,
thus showing changeless consciousness.

With consciousness shown clarified, *from*
pure knowledge shines as deathlessness. *11*

Nothingness seems blind and dark;
apparent being can deceive. *from*
Yet each of these has its own use. *12-13*

Nothingness of passing things
can lead away from change and death,
thus showing being's changeless self.

Its changelessness shown clarified, *from*
pure being shines as deathlessness. *14*

The face of truth seems veiled in light.
But this apparent veil dissolves *from*
when light is known as truth itself. *15*

From knowing light comes all control
and progress in the seeming world.
It is the single radiant source
where outward-seeming rays are joined.

May I turn back from outward light,
to find this shining principle *from*
which is the truth I am within. *16*

May mind and body be revealed
as object-things which have no life.

May life be truly realized
as unconditioned consciousness, *from*
where self and world are known as one. *17*

As seeming life pursues its course,
unknowingly or knowingly
in search of happiness and truth,

may mind turn back to its own source,
destroying ego's pettiness *from*
to find the truth I really am. *18*

From the Prashna Upanishad

Matter and life

From where does this creation rise?

In our experience, all creation
rises from duality
of *matter* known by knowing *life*.

These two are like the moon and sun.
The moon appears reflecting light
that comes from outside: from the sun.
But sun appears through burning light
that comes from its own source within.

So too, dead matter must be known
by light which shines from something else.

That something else is knowing life,
which shines by light from self within.

It's from this inner source of light,
within each personality,
that all created things arise.

And where this inner source is found, *from*
undying truth is realized. *1*

Living faculties

Which faculties support creation?

Which illuminate experience?

Do they manifest a common,
underlying principle,
which is essential to them all?

In everyone's experience,
the whole created world depends:

upon identifying things,
upon observing form and change,
upon interpreting what's meant,
upon comparing qualities,
on understanding time and space
continuing through different things.

And all these faculties depend
upon our senses, speech and minds,
illuminating what we see.

Seen from the world, it thus appears
that life and consciousness depend
on various different faculties.

But truly seen, this is not so;
for all illumination comes,
through life, from consciousness within.

Wherever living consciousness
is seen to leave this shell of body,
so are mind and speech and senses
and all living faculties:
as though a swarm of bees were
following their queen, out from a hive.

Our faculties all shine by light
of consciousness that lives within.
It's the essential principle
on which, in truth, they all depend.

But it does not depend on them,
because it shines by its own light.

In truth, it manifests itself,
and thus all seeming faculties, *from*
creating the apparent world. *2*

Learning from experience [1]

From where does sentient life arise?

How is it here within the body,
how expressed in body's acts?

How does it seem divided here
in different living faculties?

How does it lead beyond the body?
How does it go out to world?

And how does it come back to self? *from 3.1*

Each person's life is born from self,
appearing like a moving image
drawn by mind on consciousness.

Through this activity of mind,
life is expressed in body's acts. *from 3.3*

As life expresses consciousness,
it carries out its purposes
through various different faculties
that are divisions of itself. *from 3.4*

One of these faculties reacts
to objects that have been perceived:
discarding waste, restricting aims,
and thus creating partial views
of world, as it appears perceived.

A second of these faculties
looks on from what is now perceived:
projecting choices, from the past,
through life that carries on in time.

[1]See *Interpreting the Upanishads*, pages 83-91, for an indication of how most of this retelling interprets the original text (in particular 3.3-12).

A third among these faculties
assimilates perceptions and
interpretations into knowledge
at the background of the mind:
where what is known is understood.
There, silent understanding knows,
unmoved by passing wants and needs
noised out by wish and fantasy.

A fourth among the faculties
goes circulating back and forth,
contrasting and comparing things:
thus judging valued qualities
and spreading subtle influence.

A fifth among the faculties
expresses understanding which
has come from past experience: so *from*
that learning may continue on. *3.5-7*

These different faculties relate
to different aspects of the world
that everyone experiences.

External choice that's mere reaction
corresponds to narrow objects
which attention has selected
from a world of many things.

Intention looking on through time
relates to processes of change,
by which all objects have been formed
and all objectives are achieved.

Understanding corresponds
to underlying principles,
continuing through change and difference
in the world's appearances.

Discerning judgement corresponds
to qualities and values that
our feelings judge and thoughts compare
in the world that mind conceives.

Expression rising from within
is manifest in outer world
by living energy of change:
which burns what's happened in the past, *from*
thus forming new experiences. *3.8-9*

Each moment of our changing lives,
we come to life conditioned by
those influences from the past
that lead on to our future lives.

Whatever's learnt is thus reborn
from death of past experiences,
as seeming life keeps cycling on *from*
from death to birth and birth to death. *3.10*

But underlying seeming life
conditioned by appearances,
what is the unconditioned ground
where life arises and returns
and living truly is alive?

By questioning relentlessly
towards this unconditioned ground,
the self that knows all life is known *from*
and deathless truth is realized. *3.11-12*

What lives in sleep? [2]

When waking world dissolves in sleep,
how is a person still alive?

When waking senses fall asleep,
what is it that remains alive:

perceiving dreams as they arise,
and knowing unconditioned peace
as dreams dissolve in depth of sleep?

What common ground of life is shared
by all our different faculties?

What common, living principle
continues on, through changing states
of waking sense and dreaming mind, *from*
into the peace of dreamless sleep? *4.1*

At evening, when the setting sun
withdraws from sky, it takes its rays
of light with it; so darkness falls,
till morning, when the sun appears
and brings its light again with it.

So too in sleep, when mind withdraws
from outside world, it takes all sense
of world with it; so that a sleeping
person does not see or hear
or smell or taste or feel the world *from*
in which the sleeping body lies. *4.2*

Thus, when a person falls asleep,
the senses are withdrawn in mind:
which does not now go out to world,
but only sees its own perceptions,
thoughts and feelings in its dreams.

[2]See *Interpreting the Upanishads*, pages 119-121, for an indication of how part of this retelling interprets the original text (in particular 4.9-10).

Though outer senses are dissolved,
the fires of mind may still be burning,
forming dream appearances:

of seeming objects and reaction,
processes and willed intention,
qualities, interpretation,
principles of understanding,
living energy expressing *from*
learning from experience. *4.3-4*

And here in dreams the mind expands:

recalling previous sights and sounds,
imagining new sights and sounds;
reliving past experiences,
creating new experiences;

thus working out what carries over
from the stores of past experience
to the dream and waking worlds
imagined and conceived by mind.

Within the world of dreaming mind,
it's only mind that dreams the world
and mind is all the world that's dreamt.

Mind dreams what's seen and is not seen.
It dreams what's heard and is not heard.
It dreams what's felt and is not felt.
It dreams what's there and is not there.

The dreaming mind knows all it dreams,
and it is all that's known in dream.

In truth, it only knows itself,
unmixed with any other thing.

Beneath each dream's appearances,
mind is in truth pure consciousness: *from*
whose only being is to know. *4.5*

When mind returns to its own being
underlying all its dreams,
it is dissolved in consciousness
where no appearances are found.

This is the state of dreamless sleep
and unaffected happiness:
where living actions come to rest, *from*
absorbed into their common ground. *4.6*

Like birds returning home to roost,
all living faculties return
to underlying consciousness: *from*
the knowing self in each of us. *4.7*

This underlying consciousness
is here in all experiences.

It is the principle that knows:

all objects, matter, forms and change,
all symbols, meaning, valued
qualities and character, all
principles and continuity;

all sight and what there is to see,
all hearing and what's to be heard,
all smell and what there is to smell,
all taste and what there is to taste,
all touch and what is there to touch;

all speech and what there is to say,
all grasp and what is to be grasped,
all creativity and what
there is to make and to enjoy,
all waste and what must be disposed,
all movement and where it might go;

all sense of self and what there is
to be identified as self,
all will and what is to be willed,
all thought and what there is to think,
all feeling and what's to be felt,
all life and all it can express.

All knowing and what's there to know *from*
are known by light of consciousness. *4.8*

It is the inner principle
of all our different faculties.

It lights all seeing from within.
It's that which is aware in touch.
From it, all meaning is expressed;
it shows all meaning heard in sound.
And it discerns all taste and smell.

It is the thinking principle,
the knowing subject of the mind:
which carries on through passing states,
as thoughts and feelings come and go.

It is the common principle
within a person's changing acts.

And thus, for everyone, it is
the changeless self that carries on
through all the different acts it knows.

It's for this self that acts are done.

This principle of knowing self
is what each person really is.
from
It's that which everyone calls 'I'. *4.9*

It has no image in itself.
Nor has it any kind of body,
nor conditioned qualities.

As pure, unchanging consciousness,
it is the unconditioned ground
of all conditioned faculties
and all the world that they perceive.

Whoever comes to know this self
finds all the world's reality *from*
and realizes everything. *4.10*

Contemplation and its results

What is the use of contemplation?
In the end, where does it lead?

After so much time and effort
has been spent in search of truth, *from*
what state of being is achieved? *5.1*

There are three stages in this search, *from*
described within the symbol 'Om'. *5.2*

The letter 'a' is first conceived
to represent the waking state:
where truth is sought outside, and leads *from*
to body's being in the world. *5.3*

The letter 'u' is next conceived
to represent the state of dream:
where mind creates what it perceives,
located somehow in between
an inner self and outer world.

If 'a' and 'u' are spoken joined
together, the result is 'o'.[3]

So too, when dream experiences
are taken into count, along
with waking sense of outside world,
then truth is sought in subtle mind;

thus leading to a mediating
state, of going back and forth *from*
between what knows and what is known. *5.4*

[3]In Sanskrit, the letter 'a' is pronounced as '-er' in 'father', and the letter 'u' is pronounced as 'u' in 'full'. If this short 'a' and short 'u' are first pronounced separately and are then progressively run together, it can be seen that they combine to form the sound 'o' (as in 'home'). Hence, 'o' is conceived to be made up of 'a' and 'u'.

The letter 'm' comes last, and
represents the state of dreamless sleep:
where neither world nor mind appears.

If 'a' and 'u' and 'm' are spoken
joined together in one sound,
the single word they make is 'Om'.

So too, when our experience of
deep sleep is taken into count,
along with dream and waking states;

then truth is sought in consciousness
beneath all mere appearances
of waking world and dream and sleep.

In depth of sleep, pure consciousness
shines as it is: quite free of all
appearances superimposed
on it, by partial body, sense
and mind, in waking state and dream.

This unconditioned consciousness,
that's seen unmixed in dreamless sleep,
continues on through all experience:

lighting all appearances,
and shining by itself, unchanged,
when no appearances arise.

It is the deathless principle
that lives in body, sense and mind;
beyond all our conditioned lives,
unaffected by all ills.

Whoever knows it sheds all ill, *from*
just as a snake casts off its skin. *5.5*

Each state of waking, dream or sleep
gives on to other states and thus,
in course of time, must change and die.

But something in us stays alive:
continuing through changing states,
co-ordinating different acts
that go outside or come back in
or cycle back and forth between.

By knowing this that lives in us,
a person finds stability *from*
and is not shaken off from truth. *5.6*

Thus contemplation finally
leads on, beyond all changing states,
to unconditioned, timeless peace *from*
untouched by fear or age or death. *5.7*

Human existence

What is this human being that *from*
appears made up of different parts? *6.1*

Right here, in body, sense and mind,
this human being can be found. *from*
In it, these different parts arise. *6.2*

It seems to rise itself, through various
outward-going faculties
that form experience of the world.

But, seen more truly, it remains
unchanged, as the established base
on which all faculties depend, *from*
as they are seen to act and change. *6.3*

From it comes life, from life belief,
hence time and space, and quality,
illuminating energy,
transforming shapes, and different things
perceived by body, sense and mind.

Thus body, sense and mind arise,
and sustenance that they consume.

From sustenance come strength and purpose,
means and actions, and hence worlds
made up of different-seeming things *from*
identified by different names. *6.4*

All flowing rivers are just water,
like the sea to which they come.

But in the sea where they all join,
their separate-seeming names and forms
are all dissolved; and water is
then manifest, just as it is:

in its unconditioned state
beneath all seeming name and form.

So too, all different-seeming parts
of changing personality
are nothing else but consciousness:

just like this human being that
they're understood to constitute,
when they are seen as joined in one.

Here, in this common 'human-ness',
their separate-seeming names and forms
are all dissolved; and consciousness
is manifest, just as it is:

in its unconditioned state
beneath all seeming name and form.

Hence, that which first appears perceived
as changing personality,
made up of parts, turns out to be
pure consciousness: which has no parts *from*
and does not suffer change or death. *6.5*

As moving spokes are joined and fixed
just at the centre of a wheel;

so too all changing parts of
personality are joined and fixed
in unconditioned consciousness,
here at the centre of all life.

In truth, each person is just this.

When this is known, there's no more death
and no disturbance can arise. *from*

There's only truth and nothing else. *6.6-7*

From the Muṇḍaka Upanishad

Knowing and being [1]

Complete knowledge

The great householder Shaunaka
was blessed with an enquiring mind,
unsatisfied by partial truth.

He thought: 'In this vast universe,
there are so many different things
our minds and senses seem to see.

'In each perception we perceive,
so little of the world seems shown.

'As mind and sense perceive the world
they show us small appearances,
which change from changing points of view.

'A mountain seen from far seems small;
from closer up it grows in size.

'A person on the lower slopes
sees grass and trees, hears rustling leaves,
smells flowers, feels the warmth of sun;

'but higher up stark cliffs appear,
with craggy shapes of barren rock,
and eerie sounds of rushing wind,
and scentless feel of chilly air.

'And yet, these different seeming things
are varying appearances
through which one mountain can be known.

[1]See *Interpreting the Upanishads*, pages 30-36, 199-200, 111-115 and 145-148, for an indication of how parts of this retelling interpret the original text (in particular: 1.1.3-9, 1.2.12-13, 2.1.1-10 and 3.1.1-2, respectively).

'So too, in all experience,
the many things we seem to see
are differing appearances
through which we know one universe.

'What is this one same universe
in which our minds and senses see
so many different seeming things?

'Is there some way to understand
this one complete reality
we know through all appearances
of everything that seems to be?'

So Shaunaka, with due respect,
approached the teacher Angiras
and asked: 'Can knowledge of the world's
reality be so complete
that all the many things we seem
to see are understood in it?

'Can something so complete be found *from*
that knowing it knows everything?' *1.1.3*

'The truth you seek,' said Angiras,
'is plain to see, and can be found
by anyone who wishes it.

'To know it you must go beyond
all scriptures, sciences and arts:
for these are mere constructions, made
by partial body, sense and mind.

'Beneath all learned structures, built
of form and name and quality,
upon what basis do we join
the partial views of sense and mind,
to make our knowledge more complete?

'This basis must be firm. It must
remain: while mind and body change,
and changing views give rise to sights,
sensations, feelings, thoughts that come *from*
and go in our experience. *1.1.4-5*

'It is no object seen by mind
and sense; for all such objects come
into experience when they
are seen, and go away again
as our attention turns elsewhere.

'Unseen by sense, unseen by mind,
it is the knowing basis which
must carry on, continuing
through changing sense and changing mind,
as seeming objects come and go.

'It is not body, sense or mind,
for these are merely instruments
of change and action in the world.

'It is no object that can act
on other objects; nor can it
be acted on, by anything.

'It has no family, nor class;
nor has it eyes that see, nor ears
that hear, nor hands that touch or hold,
nor feet that stand or walk or run.

'It does not act; it only knows.

'It is pure consciousness: which lights
up all appearances that come
and go in our experience.

'All space, all time, all difference,
all change are known by consciousness.
Thus space and time and difference
and change cannot apply to it.

'It is the undivided base
from which divided space is known,
the unity in difference,
the changeless continuity
which knows all change and passing time.

'It's always here, in every one
of us, each moment that we know;

'whatever we may seem to know,
whatever it may seem we do
not know, or only know in part.

'Upon this base of consciousness,
all objects are perceived and thus
are manifested in the world.

'In consciousness, all seeming things
arise, exist and come to end.

'Beneath gross things of outer sense,
beneath all subtleties of mind,
it is creation's changeless source:

'from which all seeming things come forth,
on which each seeming thing depends, *from*
to which each thing returns again. *1.1.6*

'As from a spider thread comes forth
and is drawn in, or just as plants
grow out of earth and when they die
dissolve in earth again; so too
all things that we perceive, throughout
the manifested universe,

'arise from changeless consciousness,
are manifest as consciousness
taking on apparent form,
and when they end are shown dissolved *from*
as nothing else but consciousness. *1.1.7*

'Each moment of experience,
a person's mind and sense perceive
a partial view that seems to show
some object in the universe.

'At different times, through different minds,
through different capabilities
of sense, we seem to see a vast
variety of different things.

'And thus it seems that we perceive
a universe of vast extent,
containing more complexity
than sense or mind can comprehend.

'In this vast-seeming universe,
our little senses only see
small objects, each a little piece
of matter formed in space and time.

'When objects interact, we see
the energy that they exchange;
and thus material things seem formed
of subtle energy that flows,
through space and time, to manifest
the outward world our senses see.

'If outward things are seen as forms
of manifesting energy,
then what is thus made manifest?

'What do forms mean? How can they be
interpreted, to understand
more than our senses seem to see?

'Forms are interpreted by mind:
which is expressed in forms,
and which reflects within itself
to ask for truth that forms express.

'Where mind turns back towards its source,
it is dissolved in consciousness;
which has no parts, nor suffers change.

'There, partiality and change
do not apply; and thus complete,
undying truth is realized.

'But where the mind is turned towards
an outer world of seeming things,
there only partial truths are seen, *from*
expressed by mind in outward acts. *1.1.8-9*

Good acts

'Through scriptures, sciences and arts,
we learn good acts that lead to good
results, for the prosperity *from*
of mind and body in the world. *1.2.1-6*

'But such prosperity is not
complete, nor is it permanent;

'for minds and bodies change and die,
as limited, uncertain parts
of a much larger universe.

'Physical and mental acts,
however good and wise they seem,
are only passing means we use
and leave behind, in search of truth.

'Whoever looks for happiness
in mind's and body's passing acts *from*
goes on to suffer age and death. *1.2.7*

'Whatever mind appears to know
is never more than partly true.

'Mind's truth is mixed with ignorance,
and thus seems changed as different things
appear from different points of view.

'When people pride their minds as wise,
forgetting what mind does not know,
they wander, blind to ignorance
that leads them blindly on and on,
from change to change, from death to death, *from*
from suffering to suffering. *1.2.8*

'When acts achieve desired goals,
mind thinks it has achieved success.
But such attachment to mere acts
and their results does not bring truth.

'When one desire is satisfied,
the mind soon longs for something else;

'and thus, new partiality
again distorts what mind perceives,
again taints truth with falsity,
again makes life seem compromised
by faults and wrongs and miseries.

'Attached to passing goals and acts,
our minds seem bound to seek escape
from one distraction to the next, *from*
from restlessness to restlessness. *1.2.9-10*

'But when our minds reflect on truth,
we seek impartiality,
beneath the partial points of view
that vary with our changing acts.

'Then, mind's distractions are restrained
and faculties become composed;
as mind returns, dispassionate,
to that same source from where it comes,
to its own base of consciousness.

'From this impartial source of truth
arises everything we know.
To this we turn unknowingly
for everything we wish to know.

'Whoever seeks this common source
must find a teacher who will show
unchanging truth in seeming change,
the deathless centre of all life *from*
that each of us experiences. *1.2.11-13*

The unborn source

'As sparks come forth from blazing fire;
so too our many seeming lives
arise from one same consciousness,
shine out as only consciousness,
and as they seem to fade away *from*
leave nothing else but consciousness. *2.1.1*

'This principle of unmixed light
shines out unchanged from deep within
each changing form of bodied life,
gives life to every breath we take,
and lights the seeming world outside.

'It has itself no bodied form.
It has no birth. It has no breath.
It has no mind, nor faculties.

'It is beyond all we conceive *from*
as here or there, or anywhere. *2.1.2*

'From it is born all life, all mind,
all feeling, thought, perception, sense,
all principles, all qualities,
all meanings, all the changing forms
and all the many varied things *from*
of which the universe seems made. *2.1.3*

'The world is known by consciousness;
the world is seen by consciousness;
all meanings are but consciousness;
all qualities are consciousness;

'and everything that feelings feel,
or thoughts conceive, or senses see,
is nothing else but consciousness.

'The world stands but in consciousness,
which is each person's real self.

'The blazing sun is consciousness;
the moon's cool light is consciousness;
dark clouds and rain are consciousness;
the solid earth and all the crops
and food it bears are consciousness.

'And all the many, varied forms
of life we creatures seem to lead,
here born and fed upon the earth, *from*
are only forms of consciousness. *2.1.4-5*

'From consciousness comes all we say,
all that we do, all we express,
all speech, all poetry, all song,

'all acts, intentions, purposes,
all we perceive or think or feel,
all energy, vitality, *from*
all justice, truth and happiness. *2.1.6-8*

'Upon this base of consciousness,
great-seeming mountains are perceived,
and different rivers seem to flow
through different regions of the earth
to join the oceans' vast expanse.

'In consciousness all forms arise:
all object-forms, all forms of life,
all solid things, all changing flow,
all gross and subtle elements
of body and of mind in which *from*
we seem to find our inner selves. *2.1.9*

'This principle of consciousness,
this single principle alone
is all there is: all of the world
our outward senses seem to see,

'all action in this outside world,
all purpose that may be expressed,
all meaning that our thoughts conceive,
all value that emotion feels.

'This deathless, final principle
of consciousness is here and now
within each heart: for each of us,
the centre of experience.

'Whoever realizes it *from*
undoes all seeming ignorance. *2.1.10*

The unmoved centre

'Self-evident within the heart,
as consciousness that carries on
while thoughts and feelings come and go;

'it also is reality, which is the same
no matter how it may be viewed.

'It is complete reality,
unlimited by time and space:
the final, unconditioned base
of all conditions in the world;
still centre of all moving things,
all living forms, all passing time.

'Whatever seems reality,
whatever unreality,
all that you need to understand
is pure, unchanging consciousness:
the resting place on which you stand.

'It is the centre of the heart:
which all our longings truly seek, *from*
but cannot reach through sense or mind. *2.2.1*

'Self-luminous, subtler by far
than anything which mind can grasp,
it is contained entirely
in every smallest particle
that can be seen or be conceived.

'And yet, it holds within itself
the whole expanse of seeming world:
including all that world contains,
all greatness, all complexity.

'It is plain truth, uncompromised;

'unshakable reality;

'the common principle of life
that lives in every living breath,
that speaks in every word and act,
that knows each changing state of mind.

'This deathless truth is what you are. *from 2.2.2*

'Where words are used to tell of truth,
they're like a bow from which is sent
a seeker's sharp enquiry.

'To use the bow, the mind draws back
into itself, and aims itself
at its own source, where mind dissolves *from*
in unconditioned clarity. *2.2.3-4*

'From consciousness is woven sky
and earth and everything between.
From consciousness is woven mind
and all life's various functionings.

'This is the bridge to deathlessness.

'Beyond all else, cling on to truth: *from*
that self is unmixed consciousness. *2.2.5*

'As in a wheel whose spokes revolve
about the centre where they join,
so too all feelings, thoughts and acts
revolve about pure consciousness,
still centre where all joins in one.

'It's here that differences begin,
and here that differences must end.

'It's here that movement seems to start
and come to rest in peace again.

'Think of this only as your self *from*
and cross all dark to light beyond. *2.2.6*

'It is the knowing principle
in all that's known, all that is learned:

'source of all greatness in the world,
the shining background of the heart,
mind's essence guiding body's life, *from*
standing firm as self within. *2.2.7*

'When mind dissolves in happiness,
the nature of the self shines clear:
as pure, unclouded consciousness.

'The steadfast see it everywhere. *from 2.2.8*

'When it is seen in good and bad,
in high and low, in far and near;

'all knots of heart become untied,
all doubts dissolve, no action binds. *from 2.2.9*

'In every personality,
it is the shining inner core:
untroubled, partless, absolute.

'Pure light that lights all seeming light,
It only can be known as self:
where known and knower are but one. *from 2.2.10*

'It is not lit by sun or moon
or stars or lightning in the sky
or any kind of alien fire.

'It shines alone, by its own light.
Its very nature is to shine.

'Whatever light is seen to shine
must shine by light of consciousness. *from 2.2.11*

'This one complete reality
of unmixed, deathless consciousness
is here in front; it is behind;
it's on the right and on the left,
above, below, and everywhere.

'It's all there is, in all the world:
the final goal of all desire. *from 2.2.12*

Ego, self and truth

‘What really is a person’s self
that lives in body, senses, mind?

‘It seems to relish pleasant things;
it seems to suffer misery.

‘It seems a separate ego in
an outside world, conditioned by
the fruits of world’s activities.

‘Such ego, acting in the world,
enjoying pleasure, suffering pain,
is just a little piece of world,
consuming fruits of worldly acts.

‘It’s just an object in the world.
It cannot really be the self.

‘The self is that in us which knows.

‘When body seems to know the world,
it is called “self”. But when it seems
that body is an instrument
through which perceiving senses know,
then senses seem to be the self.

‘Next, when it seems that senses are
but instruments of knowing mind,
then mind appears to be the self.

‘And finally, when mind is seen
to be a mere activity
which forms appearances of world,

‘the self is known for what it is:
pure consciousness, which does not act
but only lights appearances.

‘This light is no activity
which starts or runs its course or ends
or is conditioned by the world.

'As world's appearances are formed
by changing mind, they come and go;
but every one of them is lit
by consciousness, which always must
remain, throughout experience.

'It is the nature of the self,
whose very being is to know. *from 3.1.1*

'Appearing caught in changing acts,
a person gets depressed and
suffers misery: misunderstanding
as poor ego's helplessness
the non-possessing nature of
the real self, which does not act
and has no powers or faculties.

'But where the self is truly seen,
transcending ego: as the
unconditioned centre of all life,
all love, all happiness; there one
is free, from ego's self-inflicted
pettiness and misery. *from 3.1.2*

'Where self is seen as consciousness,
unfading source of all there is;
there vice and virtue fade away,
true unity is realized. *from 3.1.3*

'When truth is known as life itself,
which shines from every seeming thing;
what need is there for argument?

'All joy and love is found in self.
What else could be more practical? *from 3.1.4*

'This truth of self can be attained
by plain and simple honesty,
by purpose that will not give up,
by turning mind back to its source
where truth is known impartially.

'In search of truth, all faults are burned; *from*
to show pure light, unstained within. *3.1.5*

'Nothing else but truth prevails.
Whatever fails cannot be true.

'Truth is the way to reach the goal
of each desire we seem to feel.

'That goal is truth and truth alone. *from 3.1.6*

'Unlimited by any bounds,
far subtler than all subtlety,
self shines as unconditioned light,
beyond the furthest reach of thought.

'Yet it is here in every heart, *from*
immediate, in each of us. *3.1.7*

'Unseen by eyes, unsaid by speech,
unperceived by any sense,
beyond the reach of any act
that any faculty performs
or any purpose mind intends;

'this partless absolute is known
only by grace of truth itself, *from*
through pure, impartial questioning. *3.1.8*

'True self is only known by its
own consciousness, which is itself.

'The seeming consciousness of sense
is mixed with alien-seeming things.
The seeming consciousness of mind
seems mixed with changing qualities.

'When consciousness is clarified,
by seeing it for what it is, *from*
the nature of the self shines out. *3.1.9*

'In all desires for fortune, power,
prosperity, well-being, joy;
all that is sought is only self.

'Whoever realizes self
attains to purity of truth,
sees shining light in everything,
attains the goal of all desire.

'The way to true prosperity *from*
is truth made plain by one who knows. *3.1.10*

Attainment to the impersonal

'Whoever knows plain truth has reached
the final ground on which we stand:
where world is seen as only light,
as nothing else but consciousness.

'This consciousness is not the flux
of changing mind; it is the base
upon which changes come and go.

'It is the changeless background of
all changing thought: the background that
continues on as things appear
and disappear, through all the
many differing appearances
that are perceived by shifting mind.

'It is the common principle
which each calls "I", impersonal
within each personality.

'The steadfast seeker, undeterred
by petty ego's foolish fears,
pays heed to this one principle,
becomes desireless and goes *from*
beyond all birth and change and death. *3.2.1*

'By longing thought for things desired,
a person is born here or there.

'But one who is established in
the real self is self-fulfilled;
and no desire for alien things *from*
can any more cause misery. *3.2.2*

'This changeless self cannot be reached
by preaching words or learned forms,
nor by any mental act.

'By simple love for truth alone *from*
is self revealed for what it is. *3.2.3*

'It can't be reached by giving up
brute force, nor by strength of purpose,
nor passionate intensity,
nor turning back from outward show.

'Instead, all these are merely means
through which love leads to truth of self, *from*
true home of all reality. *3.2.4*

'A sage is one who knows the self
for what it is, who has no trace
of ego that identifies
the self with body or with mind.

'Fulfilled, content with what is known,
dispassionate, at peace, a sage
remains unshakably at one
with self and all reality;
wherever mind and body seem *from*
to be, no matter what seems known. *3.2.5*

'An aspirant is one who won't
be satisfied with partial truths
that rest on false identity
of self with body or with mind.

'Renouncing ego's falsities,
a seeker strives for clarity
and certainty of final truth,
beyond half-truths that ego knows.

'Each seeker, in the end, breaks free
to deathlessness, unlimited *from*
by seeming bounds of space and time. *3.2.6*

'Where true reality is found,
all seeming things are seen dissolved
back in the ground from which they come.

'This is the ground which *is* and *knows*:
where all our many seeming acts
are seen as only consciousness. *from*

'To changeless self, all things are one. *3.2.7*

'As flowing rivers join the sea,
where name and form become dissolved;
so too, when self is realized,
no bonds of name and form remain.

'Beyond obscuring differences,
the common, radiant principle *from*
of living freedom is attained. *3.2.8*

'Whoever knows the absolute
illuminates all those around
from that one centre of all things,
beyond all seeming sin and grief:

'where knots of heart dissolve in light,
where final freedom is attained, *from*
and deathlessness is realized. *3.2.9*

From the Māṇḍūkya Upanishad

The word 'Om' [1]

The word that's spoken out as 'Om',
when rightly understood, shows all
experience: all that is, all that
ever was, all that will be.

And thus it shows unchanging truth;
which stays the same, beyond all time, *from*
in everything that seems to be. *1*

Within each person's mind and heart,
while objects seem to come and go,
the self that knows all seeming change
must carry on. It's always here,
in everything we seem to know.

This self is all reality.

Reality and self, though one,
seem to appear as different things, *from*
in different states of consciousness. *2*

The outside world seems to appear
in what we call the 'waking state'.

Here, consciousness seems outward bound:
from self, through little body's gross
perceptions, out into a world
containing all our bodies and
the many other object-things *from*
our outward senses seem to know. *3*

[1]See *Interpreting the Upanishads*, pages 173-179, for an indication of how this retelling interprets the original text.

But when attention seems to turn
back in, away from outside things,
to thoughts and feelings in our minds,
another state appears, called 'dream'.

Here, consciousness remains within
our minds; and all that can appear
are subtle forms of changing mind, *from*
created by imagining. *4*

When mind subsides and dreams dissolve,
there comes a state we call 'deep sleep':
where seeming things do not appear.

Here, consciousness is shown for what
it is, unmixed with seeming things,
beneath all mere appearances
of name and form and quality.

In depth of sleep, all bonds are loosed.
All conflicts, all divisions end.

Thus, consciousness is clarified;
and its true nature shines as peace,
as undivided unity, *from*
as unconditioned happiness. *5*

All things are known by consciousness.

It is the underlying ground:
from which all seeming things arise;
on which they stand, relate together,
are controlled; and finally, *from*
in which all seeming things dissolve. *6*

Since consciousness continues through
all states that we experience;

it can't in truth be called a state:
in which some seeming thing is known
or is unknown or partly known.

It is the background of all states:
the background of reality,
against which seeming things are known.

And it is also knowing self:
which lights all seeming things, by its
own self-illuminating light.

Unseen by mind or any sense,
it lights all mind and every sense,
and all that is experienced.

It is itself pure knowing light.

This is its nature as it is;
to know, it does not need to act.

Its knowledge is no kind of act:
that may be started up or stopped,
or be directed or attached
to changing objects in the world.

It only knows. It does not act.
Its knowledge is quite unattached.

It can't be grasped, nor quite expressed,
described, or pointed out, by
any physical or mental act.

The only way it can be known
is through its own self-evidence:
as the essential basis where
all differences must be resolved.

It is the source of peace and love, *from*
where self and world are known as one. *7*

Three letters, joined in single sound,
make up the word pronounced as 'Om'.
First comes the letter 'a', then 'u', *from*
then 'm'; together, they form 'Om'.[2] *8*

[2]In Sanskrit, the letter 'a' is pronounced as '-er' in 'father', and the letter 'u' is pronounced as 'u' in 'full'. If this short 'a' and short 'u' are first pronounced separately

'A' represents the waking world
that body's outward senses see.

This is the world of 'common sense',
from which we start to look for truth
that stays the same through changing views,

through various different sights and sounds
and other such appearances *from*
perceived from different points of view. *9*

'U' represents the subtle forms
we dream within our changing minds,
conceiving thoughts and fantasies
urged on by feeling and desire.

Thus we imagine high ideals,
in search of deeper, subtler truths
beneath the gross appearances *from*
our outward senses seem to see. *10*

'M' represents the merging place
where consciousness shines out as peace,
when dreams dissolve in depth of sleep.

From this pure ground of consciousness,
all qualities, all names, all forms
arise, and seem to show a world
outside our senses and our minds.

Whenever anything appears,
it must be known by consciousness.

Nothing ever can appear
without support from consciousness.

Thus, each apparent object and
the whole apparent universe
must rest upon this knowing ground
that's here, in all appearances.

and are then progressively run together, it can be seen that they combine to form the sound 'o' (as in 'home'). Hence, 'Om' is conceived to be made up of 'a', 'u' and 'm'.

And then, as world's appearances
are understood, all forms and names
and qualities return to ground, *from*
absorbed again in consciousness. *11*

The whole word 'Om' continues on
from 'a' to 'u' and then to 'm':

thus representing consciousness
which carries on through changing states
and so contains them all in one.

In this unchanging consciousness
where all appearances dissolve,

no separate ego can remain
and happiness is realized;

for self and world are known as one.

'Om' is thus non-duality:
where *truth but merges self in self* *from*
and self shines by itself, alone. *12*

From the Taittirīya Upanishad

Complete reality

What could it mean to know complete
reality, just as it is:

beneath the various partial views
that each of us seems to perceive,
through little body, sense and mind
in a much larger universe?

If all reality were known,
there would be nothing left to know.

No trace of ignorance or doubt
could then remain, to complicate
the simple, unconditioned truth
which would at last be realized.

Satyam – truth

Complete reality is thus
plain truth, uncomplicated by
the 'ifs' and 'buts' which must arise
wherever incomplete perception
shows some seeming, partial truth
that's mixed with partial falsity.

But what, in turn, is this plain truth?

It's something that is always true,
no matter what conditions or
uncertainties may seem perceived
in the apparent world around
our partial personalities.

What's always true is always real,
beneath all mere appearances.

It is that common principle
which all appearances must share,
beneath their seeming differences.

It's where appearances differ
that they betray their falsities.

What's fully real and plainly true
is shown by all appearances:
as seen in common from all different
points of view, no matter where
or when perceived, by whom or through
what faculty or state of mind.

This common principle of truth
remains the same, through all the
seeming differences and variations
of experience: as perceptions,
thoughts and feelings come and go,

creating world's appearances
in a parade of changing show
that passes through each person's mind.

Jnyānam – knowledge

What is this common principle
of truth that all experience shares
beneath the world's appearances?

At different moments of experience,
different objects are perceived
in different ways; thus giving rise
to differing appearances
in different minds, at different times.

Whatever object may be known,
however it may be perceived,
it's never there quite on its own,
in anyone's experience.

No object is experienced
without some kind of consciousness,
to light what it appears to be.

What is in fact experienced
is not an object on its own,
but object mixed with consciousness.

Hence, what's *supposed* to be an object
is, as *actually* experienced,
knowledge of the object known.

In truth, the object is not there
outside of consciousness at all.

What's there is knowledge, nothing else.

What seemed to be an object, thus,
turns out to be pure consciousness:
with nothing else mixed into it,
beneath all mere appearances.

Anantam – the infinite

This underlying consciousness
is not an act of sense or mind,
conditioned by the seeming objects
it appears to act towards.

Unlike the seeming consciousness
of partial body, sense and mind,
it does not change in course of time.

As different things seem to be known,
as different feelings, thoughts, perceptions
change apparent consciousness
of seeming objects in the world;

it is the underlying base
of unconditioned consciousness
that carries on through differences
of time and personality.

It's the essential base on which:

our lives continue on through time;
our different acts, perceptions, thoughts
and feelings can co-ordinate;

our different minds say what they mean,
and understand what other people
do or say or think or feel.

This is the base of consciousness
that's here in all experience:
no matter what may seem perceived,
no matter how, no matter where,
nor in whose mind, nor at what time.

It is the common principle
of truth that all experience shows,
the ground of all reality.

In space and time, it's infinite:

continuing through everything
quite unbegun and unconfined
by any kind of bound or end
or limit or conditioning.

And yet, to reason seeking truth,
it is quite fixed and definite,

as the essential ground of all
necessity and certainty:

first source, sole base, of all that's known,
and final end of questioning.

Complete reality is thus
plain truth of unmixed consciousness,
beyond all limiting conditions
in the objects we perceive
through partial body, sense and mind.

Known as the essence of the self
within each person's mind and heart,
it is the highest, final goal
that all desire truly seeks.

Just knowing it resolves all strife,
frees all desire, fills all need,

and realizes unity *from 2.1*
of separate-seeming self revealed *(earlier*
at one with all reality. *part)*

Levels of appearance

How does the seeming world arise
from underlying consciousness?

'Ether' – *the pervading element (ākāsha)*

It rises first through background
continuity: enabling knowledge
from the past to carry on,
so that the qualities of world
may be contrasted and compared.

'Air' – *the qualitative element (vāyu)*

Hence background continuity
gives rise to quality and character:
enabling judgement of
perceived appearances, and thus
interpreting what they might mean.

'Fire' – *the illuminating element (agni)*

Hence quality and character
give rise to meaning that illuminates
more than what is immediately
perceived: enabling a
variety of changing forms
to be imagined and described.

'Water' – *the transforming element (āpas)*

Hence meaning in its turn gives rise
to form and change: enabling objects
in the world to be identified
as separate bits of matter,
each one formed in its own way.

'Earth' – *the material element (prithivī)*

Thus form and change give rise to matter,
seen divided into objects
that together constitute
the world where body seems to live.

Living creatures *(prajās)*

Each living body is made up
of matter organized to act
towards the purposes of life.

Hence plants and living organisms
are produced, grow and subsist:
consuming and transforming matter
taken in from world outside.

Each body lives consuming food,
and is itself potential food
which in its turn may be consumed:
for other bodies to be born,
to grow, develop and subsist.

Our bodies use what they consume
to act expressing consciousness.

It's this expression that enables us
to see our bodies as alive.

From this comes personality
of living self seen from outside,
as consciousness of self is seen
expressed in outward forms and acts.

At first, this self seems to be body; *from 2.1*
made of food, and needing food *(latter*
to carry on its seeming life. *part)*

Food *(annam)*

For body, food is sustenance
found formed into the many different
bodies that the world contains.

From food consumed, all bodies have
been born; by food they live and grow;
until they end themselves as food
for other bodies to consume.

Where all the bodies in the world
are seen as only sustenance
thus taking many different forms,

there all the world's reality
may be approached as sustenance
found here within each person's self.

But here within each seeming self
of body made from food consumed,
there is another, subtler self
that makes the body seem alive.

This is the self of energy
that is expressed in living acts. *from 2.2*

Living energy *(prāṇa)*

This self of vital energy
sustains the body's seeming life.

It drives the body's acts toward
their purposes; and thus enables
body to continue as
a living organism,
functioning towards objectives of
intention, meaning and desire.

All living acts, throughout the world,
express this vital energy
that forms our personalities.

And where all living acts are seen
as its expressions in the world,

there all the world's reality
may be approached as energy
found here within each person's self.

But what is vital energy?
What makes it seem to be alive?

It only lives in that its acts
express intention, meaning, wish,
from thought and feeling in the mind.

Hence vital energy itself
expresses life from mind within;

and thus it forms a seeming self
in which another, subtler self –
made up of mind that thinks and feels –
is more essentially alive. *from 2.3*

Mind *(manas)*

In everyone's experience,
as mind's perceptions, thoughts and feelings
come and go, they form a changing
stream of world's appearances.

But through this stream of passing show,
there is an underlying consciousness
that carries on; thus knowing
change and difference, comparing
and contrasting qualities:

discerning good from bad, and right
from wrong, and truth from falsity.

All mind's perceptions, thoughts and feelings
rise expressing consciousness,
with its discernment of what's good
and right from what is bad and wrong.

And this discerning consciousness
is what gives value, meaning, life
to the appearances mind forms.

So, just as vital energy
expresses mind, the mind in turn
expresses knowing consciousness
that gives the mind its seeming life.

Thus mind too forms a seeming self
in which another, subtler self –
of consciousness that knows apart – *from*
is more essentially alive. *2.4*

Discerning consc- iousness *(vijnyānam)*

In everyone's experience,
this consciousness continues on
through all the world's appearances.

Beneath these world appearances,
it's shared in common by them all:

the changeless common ground on which
what's known continues on through time,
and different minds communicate.

It is the common principle
of all experience: expressed
in everything that we perceive,
in everything we think and feel.

It is complete reality,
beneath all mere appearances.

Thus known complete, quite unconfused
with partial body, sense and mind,
it leads to non-duality:

where separate-seeming self dissolves,
and truth of self is realized — *from*
at one with all reality. — *2.4*

Happiness
(ānanda)

Hence consciousness that knows apart
leads finally to what self is:

pure, unconditioned happiness
where lack and want cannot arise;

because the knowing self, in truth,
is one with all reality,
and there is nothing else besides.

Discernment, mind and energy
and bodies' actions all express
this ultimate, non-dual self.

Within each personality, — *from 2.5*
it's the essential, living core — *and be-*
of unconditioned happiness — *ginning*
that cannot change or pass away. — *of 2.6*

Nothingness

Since body, sense and mind are only
partial instruments, they can't
perceive complete reality.

They can't see everything at once,
there's always something left to see.

Each object that they see is part
of something more than what is seen:
part of a larger universe.

Each of their objects is thus always
limited and incomplete.
It's just a part appearance of
a more complete reality.

No object then in truth exists,
in its own right. It is a mere
appearance, shown by partial sight
that doesn't fully see what's there.

But does 'complete reality'
itself exist? If it's not seen
by any body, sense or mind,
how can we know it's truly there?

Should we conclude that there is no
reality at all, but only
meaningless appearances
that show us empty nothingness?

Such a conclusion would be wrong,
for there's a contradiction here.

If all reality is known
not to exist, then that which knows
does not exist and cannot know.

So nothingness refutes itself,
and leads us on to ask again
how we might know reality.

If all reality is known
as that which truly and completely
is, beneath what partially
appears; then that which knows this truth
must also be completely real.

The self which knows reality
cannot itself be just some part
appearance of what's really there.
It must be all reality.

It is at once the knowing self
and all that's ever truly known.

It's that in us which knows itself:
pure consciousness, unlimited
by seeming objects in the world
perceived by body, sense and mind.

We often leave this seeming world:

not only when the body dies,
but also when we fall asleep;

or when desires are achieved
and world dissolves in happiness;

and even every moment of
our lives, as past thought dies away,
so that new thought may rise again.

When we thus leave this seeming world,
through death or sleep or happiness
or change of thought, what happens then?

At first it seems we enter in
a state of empty nothingness,
where consciousness has disappeared.

But if there were no consciousness,
this state could not be known at all.

In truth, there's only consciousness;
it's seeming objects that aren't there.

The nothingness we seem to see
is nothingness of seeming world:
which is in truth pure consciousness,
at one with all reality.

Where there is ignorance, the world
is left behind unknowingly,
in fear of unknown nothingness
that seems to follow fading world.

Where truth is known, the world becomes
entirely irrelevant.
When it appears, it's known as only
unconditioned consciousness.

And when it disappears, it's left
behind quite knowingly: as *from*
disappearing back into this same *2.6*
self-evident reality *– first*
of unconditioned, knowing light. *part*

The creator

Creation is the work of ego,
which desires to be more
than what it thinks itself to be.

Creating ego is a self
that seems somehow dissatisfied.
It is a seeming consciousness
that feels itself inadequate.

From this dissatisfaction, it
feels need and want and loneliness.

Thus it desires to multiply,
to issue forth as many things;
so it might raise its self-esteem
and cure its self-belittlement.

Because it's sorry for itself,
it starts to dream of better
possibilities; and for a while
it even cheers itself with the
pretence of passing fantasy
that's somehow taken to be true;

until the fancy passes on
and brings more self-belittlement.

Thus ego's fancied prospects only
lure it on to feeling sorrier
for what again it's forced to take
as its own present sorry state.

By feeding on its own frustrations,
ego breeds upon itself
with spiralling intensity;

and thus, in everyone's experience,
ego's fantasies create
perceived appearances, expanding
into the entire universe
that seems to be perceived.

Creating the entire universe
from its own fantasies,
the self-deceiving consciousness
of restless ego permeates
the seeming world it thus becomes.

It is the stuff of which is made:

what's present here to body's senses
and what's thought beyond by mind;

what seems defined or left unsaid;
what seems founded or unfounded;

what seems true or seems untrue
to seeming body, sense and mind.

The whole apparent world perceived
by seeming body, sense and mind
is only ego's fantasy.

But then, what is the truth we seek
beneath the world's appearances?

What is this ego that creates
the world? What truth is there in it,
beneath its many falsities?

For every person, ego is
a seeming self, identified
with little body, sense or mind.

It's body, sense and mind that are
inherently inadequate.
They're only little parts of world
that suffer lack and need and want.

Why then are they identified
as that which each of us calls 'I'?
Why do they seem a person's self?

In everyone's experience,
the self called 'I' is that which knows.

Where sentient body seems to know
a world outside, it is called 'I'.

But when the body's seen to be
an instrument, through which the senses
see; then senses are called 'I'.

And when in turn the senses are
regarded as mere instruments
through which the mind perceives; then it's
the mind which gets to be called 'I'.

And finally, when mind as well
is seen as just an instrument
that acts to form appearances
which consciousness illuminates;

then it is unconditioned consciousness,
unmixed with body, sense
and mind, that's truly known as 'I'.

Beyond this consciousness, there's
nothing else; for it's no instrument
that acts in any way at all.

It only carries on unchanged,
self-luminous, throughout the course
of all experience, as perceptions,
thoughts and feelings come and go.

It is the changeless base from which
appearances seem to arise, *from*
on which they stand, and where they go *2.6*
as they dissolve back in their ground *– latter*
of self-illuminating light. *part*

Thus it is consciousness that is
the true identity of self.

It's just by falsely seeing
consciousness, confused with body, sense
and mind, that people call them 'I'.

The ego is only a false
identity, a false appearance
seen by ignorant mistake.

The ego isn't really there,
just like the world that it creates;
for ego is a part of world.

The seeming world is mere appearance,
risen up from mere appearance,
on the base of consciousness.

Effectively, the seeming world
creates itself; and in this sense
it may be called 'spontaneous'.

Thus nature's spontaneity,
its genuine, unprompted
'naturalness', is the essential
flavour of the whole created world.

Through all its many happenings,
the world spontaneously expresses
its own base of consciousness:
which does not act, but where all actions
rise, are based and come to rest.

Where this essential spontaneity
is understood, the world
is seen expressing consciousness:

which forces nothing, makes no effort,
does not put on any act,
and yet inspires everything.

Arriving at this spontaneity,
one comes to happiness:
where consciousness shines out, at one
with all that happens in the world.

If there were not this happiness,
here at the changeless, knowing background
of the changing object-world;
what reason could there be for
living on, or doing anything?

Without expressing consciousness,
what life or meaning could there be
in any act or happening?

It is the source of happiness:
from which all motivations rise,
on which each one of them depends,
and where they find what they desire
as they return to peace and rest.

It is each person's true support:
unseen by any sense or mind,
entirely impersonal,
undefined by word or act;

quite independent of all else,
while everything depends on it.

Thus leaving ego's fears behind
and finding one's own true support,
one goes beyond the reach of fear.

But when a person's ego picks
apparent holes in its own self;
then, for that person, there is fear.

And this is just the groundless fear
of unexamined prejudice:
of ego thinking that it knows
what it won't look at, face to face, *from*
for fear of its own ignorance. *2.7*

For fear of simple truth, before
which all the complex capabilities
of body, sense and mind
seem so inadequate, the ego
drives the seeming world that it
creates from its own restlessness.

Hence it is said: 'For fear of truth,
wind blows, sun rises, fire burns,
and lightning flashes from the sky;
as change and death drive all the world.'

But truth itself is not what's blown
about, nor made to rise, nor burned,
nor flashed like lightning from the sky.

It's unaffected happiness,
which does not change or fear or die.

from 2.8 – beginning

Kinds of happiness [1]

Imagine someone who is young,
who's open, honest, full of fun,
well-educated, sensitive,
alert, adjusted, healthy, strong,
with all the comforts wealth can bring.
Take this as 'normal' happiness.

Much more intense is happiness
of celebration, breaking free
from personal conditioning
that limits ordinary life.

And more than this, there's happiness
of settled, long experience:
which goes on bringing in rewards
for relatively many years.

But this depends on happiness
of cultivated faculties
inherited through family
and breeding in society.

And further, there is happiness
of capabilities achieved
by one's own work and discipline.

Supporting this is happiness
of mastering one's faculties:
co-ordinating and controlling
them, towards one's chosen goals.

All this is based on happiness
of aspiration to the truth,
beyond all mere appearances
of seeming objects in the world.

[1]See *Interpreting the Upanishads*, pages 158-162, for an indication of how this retelling interprets the original text.

And greater still is happiness
of coming to creation's source
from which appearances arise.

But none of these compares at all
with unconditioned happiness:

where all desires are dissolved,
and simple truth is realized *from*
that consciousness is all there is, *2.8*
with self and object known as one. *– middle*

Non-dual consciousness [2]

It's consciousness that lights
appearances, here in a person's mind.

And this same consciousness makes known
all objects in the seeming world
perceived by body, sense and mind.

Thus, inward consciousness of mind
and outward consciousness of world,
though seeming two, are only one.

As this is known, appearances
of seeming world are left behind:

withdrawing first through body-self;

then through the self of living energy
beneath the body's acts;

then through the self of mind beneath
the purposes of living acts;

then through discerning consciousness
beneath the judgements of the mind;

and thus at last to unconditioned
happiness of real self, *from*
where changeless consciousness is known *2.8*
at one with all reality. *– end*

From this all words and thoughts turn back.

For it is not attained until
they fall away, and only
consciousness remains: unlimited
by word or thought, with nothing
to obscure complete reality
where lasting happiness is found.

[2]See *Interpreting the Upanishads*, pages 158-162, for an indication of how this retelling interprets the original text.

Whoever knows this simple truth
can have no fear of anything;

nor burn with the anxiety
of asking: 'Why have I not done
what's right?' or 'Why have I done wrong?'

Both these are only ego's questions.
Neither can pertain to self.

One who knows truth is liberated
from all seeming good and ill,
superimposed by ego's ignorance *from*
upon one's own true self. *2.9*

Asking for truth [3]

Young Bhrigu, son of Varuṇa,
once asked his father: 'Sir, what's meant
when people speak, not just of some
particular apparent thing,
but of "complete reality"?'

His father said: 'Complete reality
is what appears in each
particular apparent thing,
no matter where or when perceived.

'And thus appearing differently
perceived from different points of view,
it may be seen in different ways:

'as food or sustenance, on which
each life and all the world subsists;

'as living energy expressed
in every act and happening;

'as sight or seeing, which perceives
each of the world's appearances;

'as listening, which comprehends
the meaning of what's been observed;

'as mind, which forms appearances
that come and go through course of time,
in everyone's experience;

'as speech or meaningful expression
in all acts and happenings
observed in the apparent world.

'In all these ways of seeing it,
reality is common ground
beneath all seeming differences.

[3]See *Interpreting the Upanishads*, pages 21-23 and 170-171, for an indication of how parts of this retelling interpret the original text (in particular from 3.1 and 3.6 respectively).

'The ground from which all things are born,
on which depends all that is born,
and into which all things return,
this ground is what you need to know.

'This ground is all reality.'

Then Bhrigu thought about what had *from*
been said to him, and understood: *3.1*

'Food is complete reality.

'For it's from food consumed, and thus
transmuted to some other form
by some creative process, that
all things are born into this world.

'Through processes of time and change,
it is by food consumed that things
maintain their forms and functioning,
by which they are identified.

'And when they lose their separate
identities, they come to end
as food consumed for other things
to be created and maintained.'

Reflecting thus, he asked his father
to explain a little more.

His father said: 'You need no further
words from me. You only need
to clarify what you already
know: enquiring back into
your mind with deepening
intensity; until all fancies have
been burned, and truth alone remains.

'For pure intensity of truth
itself is all reality.'

from
So Bhrigu thought a little more: *3.2*

'Perhaps it's living energy
that is complete reality.

'For all that happens in the world
is born of motivating
energy, depends on energy
as long as it continues on,
and comes to end as energy
from which new happenings arise.'

He went back to his father with
this thought, and once again was told *from*
to think some more. So now he thought: *3.3*

'Mind is complete reality.

'For every motivating purpose
and all meaning comes from mind,
depends on mind to carry on,
and comes to end in mind: from which
new purposes and meanings rise.'

Again he went back to his father,
and was told to go on asking
what was more exactly true.

And now, reflecting hard, he knew: *from 3.4*

'Complete reality is consciousness:

'which carries on through mind's perceptions,
thoughts and feelings; knowing change
and difference, and thus distinguishing
what's false from what is true.

'For all appearances arise
from this discerning consciousness,
depend on this same consciousness,
and end returned to consciousness:
where new appearances arise.'

Returning to his father with
this knowledge, he was told: 'Now ask:

'"*What is this truth of consciousness,*
when falsity has been removed?"'

Then Bhrigu realized at last: *from 3.5*

'Reality is nothing else
but unconditioned happiness:

'where falsity has been removed
from consciousness, which is thus known
at one with all reality.

'From unconditioned happiness,
rise all of our experiences.

'On it, each one of them depends.
It's what they want. It's where they go.

'It is the self that knows in us
and all we ever really know.'

from 3.6 – beginning

Sustenance

I am the sustenance consumed
by all the world of changing things.

Yet into me all changing things
and all the world become consumed.

From me, each of them issues forth,
with all their ordered functioning.

I am their deathless origin:
their common, underlying source.

Whoever freely gives of me,
is only thus accepting me.

I, who thus seem to be consumed,
am just the unaffected ground
where all consuming is consumed.

Transcending all the changing world, *from*
I'm unconditioned, knowing light. *3.10.6*

From the Shvetāshvatara Upanishad

Underlying Cause

In what sense is reality
the underlying cause from which
perceived appearances result?

And who are we that thus perceive
appearances of seeming world?

From what do we ourselves result?

How do we live? Where do we stand?

What is our basis of support,
where all our differences are joined?

As changing life swings back and forth
through passing states of joy and pain,
what stands beyond and takes us on *from*
through all our different-seeming states? *1.1*

Reality may be conceived:

as time, proceeding on through change
and thus transcending change and death;

as nature, immanent in things,
inherent in 'things-in-themselves';

as plain necessity, which can't
be otherwise than what it is;

as spontaneity, occurring
of itself, here deep within;

as elementary principle,
of which the seeming world is made;

as the originating source
from which all seeming things are born;

as consciousness, the knowing
principle of personality.

But these are different approaches,
needing to be kept apart.
For their confusion breeds the false
appearances of unreality,

with self appearing
to become what it is not.

The self that knows possesses nothing,
has itself no faculties.
It's that pure light of consciousness
which only knows and does not act.

Accordingly, it has itself
no powers or capabilities:
which act towards results that bring
us happiness or misery.

And yet, without itself performing
any act, it is the
underlying base of consciousness:

from which all capabilities
and powers rise, on which they stand,
and where they end and come to rest.

As different actions come and go,
it is their changeless, knowing base:
at once the ground from which they act *from*
and their illuminating light. *1.2*

Through meditation, harnessing
the capabilities of mind,
expanding powers are seen to rise
up from the self: which thus appears
as an almighty deity,
mysteriously concealed beneath
its own apparent qualities.

This deity is that one cause
which stands above all smaller causes,
binding things that change through time *from*
back to their source in changeless self. *1.3*

As in a wheel, the rim turns round
on moving spokes that radiate
from one, unmoving, central point;

so too this world of moving things
results from many moving causes
that themselves originate *from*
from one, unmoving, central self. *1.4*

The changing world of our experience
flows in many sensual streams,
made turbulent and tortuous by
the objects that they flow around.

And, agitated into waves
by many living energies,
this restless flow is driven on
through various faculties of mind, *from*
unhappy and dissatisfied. *1.5*

All of the lives we seem to live
and all the things that we perceive
are found contained within the flow
of passing time in our experience,
cycling round one changeless self.

In this great flow of cyclic time,
each person's life of little ego
seems confused and tossed about,
by swirling change and driving forces
petty ego can't control.

But once the knowing self is known,
distinct from that which acts in world,
then this distinction frees the ego
from the bonds that tie it down
to petty action and control.

With ego's pettiness dissolved,
the nature of the self shines out
as unaffected happiness: *from*
where harm and death do not arise. *1.6*

It's this that's worshipped as complete
and ultimate reality.

In it, that which enjoys is one
with that which is enjoyed; and both
of them are thus revealed at one
with that which motivates all change.

It is the changeless ground on which
all life and all existence stand.

It's known by those who've realized
it here within; entirely
dissolving all identity
in it: as one's own real self,
as one's own true reality.

Entirely intent on it,
they're freed from the constraining womb
of circumstance, which limits all *from*
conditioned personality. *1.7*

The worshipped deity who's called
'the Lord' is that almighty power
which brings forth all the universe:
combining change with changelessness
and what appears with what does not.

But self, possessing nothing, having
in itself no capabilities
that act in any way,
is not the world-possessing 'Lord'.

From its appearance as enjoyer
non-possessing self seems bound
to objects that appear enjoyed.

But, known as the illuminating
principle that guides all things,
the self beneath appearances
is realized as always free; with *from*
all the bonds that seem to tie it down. *1.8*

Two principles are thought unborn,
by thinking of that consciousness
which in itself knows everything
and which knows nothing but itself.

One is 'the Lord', possessing all,
with power over everything.

The other has no ownership,
does not have any powers attached
performing any kind of act.

One single unborn principle
is thought beyond duality,
by thinking of experience where
enjoyer and enjoyed unite.

In truth, the self is three in one.

It is 'the Lord', the owner of
all forms appearing everywhere.

It's also changeless consciousness,
unmixed with any kind of act.

And it is infinite, beyond
division and duality.

Here, where one finds this trinity –
of oneness holding everything,
of unconditioned consciousness,
and of non-dual happiness – *from*
reality is known complete. *1.9*

Change is the primal seed that forms
the seeming world's appearances.

Unchanging deathlessness is the
destroyer of all ignorance.

The play of change about the self
is guided and inspired by
one principle of inner light
that's called 'divine', and is in truth
the very nature of the self.

From contemplating that, from joining
into it, from truth appearing
more and more just as it is,
the world's delusions cease at last *from*
and are dissolved in peace and rest. *1.10*

Where knowing light itself is known,
all ties and limits fall away.
There all dissatisfaction ends
and neither birth nor death arise.

This is a state transcending body,
touching base with everything.

Here self shines absolute, all by *from*
itself, with all desire fulfilled. *1.11*

Here, neither time nor change is known,
but only timeless constancy
that stands entirely in self.

from
Beyond this, there is nothing else. *1.12*

Subtle powers

Just as the energy of fire
is latent in a piece of fuel;

so too the subtle energies
of life and mind are latent in
gross forms of body, seen by sense
as pieces of an outside world.

And just as fuel may be set
alight, by focused friction or
by concentrated sparks or flame;

so too the subtle powers of life
and mind may be made manifest
by meditative practices:

which concentrate intensity
within, thus setting flame to
latent energies that are not noticed
in the ordinary course
of outward life in seeming world.

These latent powers are called 'divine'
when they are used to take the mind,
beyond its usual limitations,

to that principle of light
where every limit disappears
and all the powers of mind dissolve, *from*
in unconditioned consciousness. *1.13-14*

Mental discipline

The mind is harnessed to the senses
like a chariot pulled along
by untamed horses running wild.

And it can only be controlled,
held steady on an even course,

by one who stands as consciousness: *from*
unexcited, undisturbed. *2.9*

Ego and self [1]

The surface of a mirror shows
obscurity where it is stained
by overlying dirt and dust.

But where it's cleaned, it disappears:
dissolved in its own clarity.

So too, each person's ego shows
up as an obstacle: where it
is overlaid with the impurities
of body, sense and mind,
which it identifies with self.

But when this false identity
is understood and cleared away;

then no impurities remain
and ego disappears, dissolved
in unconditioned happiness: *from*
where truth of self shines clarified. *2.14*

A person's body, sense and mind
are only instruments through which
perceptions of the world appear.

They do not know in their own right;
for their perceptions shine by light
of knowing self that lives within.

Light is the nature of the self.
Its very being is to shine:
as self-illuminating light.

It is the light of consciousness,
which lights perceived appearances
and thus illuminates the world.

[1] See *Interpreting the Upanishads*, pages 148-150, for an indication of how this retelling interprets the original text.

By looking back into the self,
one joins one's true identity:
as consciousness that knows directly,
face to face, in its own right.

And here, beneath all compromise
with mediating instruments,
one knows reality direct: *from*
unborn, unchanging, absolute. *2.15*

The universal 'Lord'[2]

God is conceived to hold the web
of circumstance, thus ruling all
the world, with powers over everything.

This universal principle,
conceived as 'God', is one alone:
in all that is created and *from*
in all that happens in the world. *3.1*

It has no second, as it stands *from*
here facing everyone within. *3.2*

It is complete reality,
unlimited and ultimate.

Found present individually
within each body, it is known
implicitly in everything.

And yet it is one single unity, *from*
containing all the world. *3.7*

This all-containing principle
is consciousness, known pictured as
the self-illuminating sun, *from*
beyond all dark obscurity. *3.8*

Beyond it, there is nothing else.

There's nothing smaller, nothing greater.
Size does not apply to it,
nor any kind of quality.

[2]See *Interpreting the Upanishads*, pages 98-105, for an indication of how this retelling interprets the original text.

The manifested universe
is like a tree which seems to grow
a multiplicity of swaying
branches, rustling leaves and flowering
blossoms seen by outward sight.

But like a tree, examined at
the trunk where it supports itself,
the many-seeming world turns out
to be a single unity,
unmoving in the changeless ground.

This changeless ground is consciousness,
where the entire seeming tree
of universal happening
dissolves in unconditioned light.

All things, in truth, are only light
pervading all experience *from*
of the entire universe. *3.9*

Transcending all appearances
perceived by body, sense and mind,
this principle of consciousness
is unattached to any form
and unaffected by all ill.

Whoever knows it does not die.
All others lead a dying life *from*
that leads to pain and misery. *3.10*

All faces, heads and bodies are
mere instruments of consciousness,
found here in every person's heart.

It is the inner principle
of spirit that pervades the world; *from*
and thus, it's worshipped as 'the Lord'. *3.11*

It is the base of changeless light
on which is founded order, justice,
goodness, harmony, and guidance *from*
towards purity and truth. *3.12*

Seen in each individual's own
experience, this principle
of consciousness is inner self:

the living centre of each
individual personality.

It's always present, living here
within each person's mind and heart;

and it is found by turning thought
to question back towards its source:
back from the world, through mind and heart, *from*
towards the source where thoughts arise. *3.13*

As feelings, thoughts, perceptions change,
pure consciousness continues on.
It is the underlying ground
that's common to each one of them,
beneath their many differences
of quality and name and form.

And it's the same for everyone,
the common ground that stays the same
beneath all change and difference.

Because it underlies all differences
of quality and name and form,
there's nothing to distinguish it
from one experience to the next
or from one person to the next.

It is the common ground on which
we understand each other's acts;
as we communicate across
our physical and mental
differences, of body and of mind.

All hearts and minds and bodies, and
all feelings, thoughts, perceptions, acts,
express this common consciousness.

All of them are its instruments,
expressing it and thereby acting
for its sake; while it remains
beyond them all, the common background *from*
of the many-seeming world. *3.14*

All that is known, throughout the world,
is only known in consciousness.

Thus, all that's known must be contained
entirely in consciousness;
and nothing really is outside.

Pure consciousness is all there is.

It's all the world's reality:
including all that's come to be
and everything that's yet to be.

It is at once the changeless light
that guides us on to deathlessness,
and the reality of world
where everything that's born and grows *from*
is fed by death of other things. *3.15*

Whatever's known expresses it,
no matter where or when perceived.

All happenings are its faculties:
expressing it and thereby acting
for its sake; while it remains
beyond them all, the changeless background *from*
of all changing happenings. *3.16*

It lights all of the qualities
that every faculty perceives:

but it is not itself attached
to any faculty at all;
for in itself it does not act.

All faculties and all their acts
depend on it to be perceived,
to focus and co-ordinate;

but it does not depend on them.

It is their central principle:
their origin and common ground,
their guiding light and stable base
enabling ordered harmony, *from*
their final goal and place of rest. *3.17*

The self that's found embodied here,
within each person, is expressed
outside as well, in nature's play
of circumstance and happening.

Remaining in itself unmoved,
it is the inner principle
from which all motivation comes.

All movements and all standing still,
no matter where or when perceived,
are understood expressing it; *from*
reflecting back to self within. *3.18*

It has no feet, yet it keeps up
with all that moves. It has no hands,
yet it grasps all experience.

It's that which sees and hears; *without*
the faculties of seeing sights
and hearing sounds, of objects in
some alien world outside itself.

It's that which knows whatever's known.

But it is *not* an object known
by anyone who knows of it
through faculties and instruments
that act towards a world outside.

Conceived as the 'I'-principle,
it's what each person really is:

pure, unconditioned consciousness,
known prior to all attributes *from*
superimposed by partial sight. *3.19*

Far subtler than all subtlety,
far greater than all magnitude
that senses see or mind conceives,
the self is found established here
in every living creature's heart.

Set free from grief and misery
by gift of grace transcending
little ego's petty purposes,
one knows the self desireless:

as that which stands beyond all acts *from*
of power and greatness in the world. *3.20*

This same unaging, ageless self
is all that's ever truly known:

perceived extending everywhere
through its pervading sovereignty.

It's spoken of as ending birth;
for where it's known all time dissolves *from*
in deathless continuity. *3.21*

The unborn[3]

That which is one cannot itself
have any qualities or other
attributes mixed into it.

And yet, through various energies
and powers that we associate
with it, one sole reality
appears expressed in many different
qualities and attributes,
which are put forth for its own sake.

It is that principle of light
in which all things are found dissolved:
right at the start, where all perception
must begin; and in the end,
when everything is said and done.

It's only from this light that mind *from*
expresses clarity of thought. *4.1*

All burning fire, all shining sun,
all subtle qualities of
atmosphere, all silver radiance of
the moon, are nothing else but this.

It's pure, complete reality:

appearing changeless in the changing
forms and states of waters' flow;

appearing in creation as *from*
'the Lord' of all that has been born. *4.2*

[3]See *Interpreting the Upanishads*, pages 145-148, for an indication of how part of this retelling interprets the original text (in particular 4.6-7).

It is each woman, every man,
each boy, each girl: whether in
crying infancy or curious
childhood, restless youth or prosperous
maturity, or in old age
that needs a staff to totter on.

Within each body that's been born,
it's called the 'individual self'.

Within all bodies, or within
the body of the universe,
it's called the 'universal self'.

It is expressed in every face:
all faces are its instruments,
displaying it for outward view *from*
to show it living here within. *4.3*

It is the dark blue butterfly;
the bright green parrot, with red eyes;
the lightning cloud; the passing seasons;
and the oceans' vast expanse.

Through its pervading sovereignty,
it lives unborn in everything:

as that which has not been begun, *from*
but where all that is born begins. *4.4*

The principle of 'nature' is
conceived unborn, but somehow
manifesting different qualities.

One is described as coloured red,
for burning energy; another
is described as coloured white,
for clarifying purity;
a third as coloured black, for darkness
or for underlying depth.

As nature manifests itself,
the many objects of the world
are born: each one its offspring, formed
from its apparent qualities.

With nature thus conceived, as
manifesting world, another unborn
principle must be conceived
along with it: as inner 'soul'
experiencing the good and bad
results of action in the world.

But then one final, unborn
principle remains to be conceived:

as consciousness which knows all change,
but is itself detached from change,
thereby illuminating good
and bad experiences that come
and go before its changeless light.

This principle of consciousness
is found entirely detached
from all the good and bad results *from*
of nature's manifesting acts. *4.5*

These principles, of inner 'soul'
and consciousness, are like two birds
conceived to live together here,
on nature's tree of happenings.

Of these two birds, one eats and tastes
the fruit, and thus becomes affected
by its qualities. The other
does not eat, but just looks on, *from*
unmoved by nature's changing acts. *4.6*

On this same tree, a person gets
depressed and suffers grief: deluded
by a sense of seeming helplessness,
and feeling thus quite dispossessed.

But when one sees what's truly loved –
as that which stands beyond all else,
as one's own boundlessness, from where
help comes, where everything belongs –
there one is freed from misery. *from 4.7*

What is the use of all the words,
techniques and capabilities
that formal learning passes on?

How can they truly be applied
in ignorance of their supporting
ground of changeless consciousness,
from which all learning is expressed?

It's only here, by knowing this
unchanging consciousness, that lasting
peace and unity are found. *from 4.8*

All world's appearances arise
in consciousness; and none of them
exists outside of consciousness.

Thus consciousness is that which holds,
within itself, all the appearances
that we perceive, of seeming
world in our experience.

The whole apparent world, conceived
through past or future thoughts and acts,
is held contained in consciousness,
from which conception seems to rise.

It's just in consciousness that
alienated ego seems to have
confined itself, by a false world
of its own fake imaginings. *from 4.9*

Creating nature, bringing all
things forth, may thus be known as
forming the appearances of world
that seems perceived by sense and mind.

And nature's uncreated 'Lord',
unlimited and infinite,
is known as changeless consciousness:
which in itself supports and holds
all changing world's appearances.

For all the world is made of things *from*
that are but part of consciousness. *4.10*

The worshipped 'Lord' who grants desires
is that single, common cause
which stands beyond each different cause.
In it, all objects come together
and disintegrate away.

Discerning it, one reaches peace *from*
that passes limits, has no end. *4.11*

It is the central origin
and basis of all faculties,
the one transcending witness of
the many-seeming universe.

It sees creation being born, *from*
as world is seeded forth from light. *4.12*

Here, in the midst of a
chaotic-seeming world of mixed-up things,
it's subtler than all subtlety:

assuming a variety
of different forms, to issue forth
as everything that is perceived.

Thus it is one reality *from*
containing all the universe. *4.14*

This all-creating principle
of light is everyone's own self:

unlimited and infinite,
found always present here at heart
in all of those that have been born.

It is conceived through mind and heart,
by turning thought and feeling back *from*
towards the source from which they rise. *4.17*

Where no obscurity remains,
there is no night and thus no day.

No false appearances create
an empty show of seeming things
that are in truth not really there.

There is no nothingness, and thus
no being that's opposed to it.
There's nothing real that could be false.

There's only changeless happiness,
uncompromised and absolute.

That's what is sought of consciousness,
the self-illuminating sun
inspiring everything within.

From it, all knowledge has come forth, *from*
right from the earliest of times. *4.18*

Not going up or down, nor
across, nor anywhere between,
could anyone catch hold of it.

It has no likeness anywhere,
nor measure to compare with it;

for it can never be contained
within the range of partial sight
perceived by outward faculties.

It is not seen by any outward
faculty; but by reflecting
back to it, through heart and mind,
to find it standing here within.

Whoever knows it thus, unborn, *from*
has come, at last, to deathlessness. *4.19-20*

Universal and individual [4]

Where knowledge is defined opposed
to ignorance that does not know,
duality is there implied:

superimposed in some mysterious,
hidden way, upon unchanging,
limitless reality.

Whatever's real is the same
no matter how it is perceived.

Thus, while appearances are changed
by different ways of seeing things,
what's true and real does not change.

As limited appearances
are changed by changing points of view,
what changes is mere ignorance:

which only sees appearances
and does not know reality,
unchanging and unlimited.

True knowledge of reality,
which knows beneath appearances,
is never changed and does not die,
no matter what appears perceived.

And here, where ignorance dissolves,
there is no more duality
of knowledge that's defined opposed
to thought of seeming ignorance.

There's nothing else but consciousness,
beyond all mind's conditioning:
beyond all mere appearances *from*
of knowledge or of ignorance. *5.1*

[4]See *Interpreting the Upanishads*, pages 150-155, for an indication of how part of this retelling interprets the original text (in particular 5.7-14).

It is the unity that stands
beyond each individual cause,
beyond the whole totality
of forms and causes in the world.

Through various kinds of knowledge, it
is all creation's ground support;

and it is also inmost light *from*
that knows perception being born. *5.2*

Web after web of manifold
illusion issues forth from it,
and is withdrawn back in again.

Thus emanating forth successively
all of creation's powers,
it is the 'Lord' of everything,
the centre of all sovereignty, *from*
unlimited and infinite. *5.3*

Just as the sun lights all directions,
upwards, downwards and between;

so too, the principle of light
that's worshipped as the highest God
is one, unchanging unity:

which stands beyond all nature's causes *from*
making different things result. *5.4*

It is the self-becoming cause
from which all things are born, on which
they're able to transform, and where
they all come to maturity.

Transcending world, it is the one
co-ordinating unity
that makes it possible for
different qualities to be arranged *from*
among world's many different things. *5.5*

Each doer acts and meets reaction,
and thus gets to be conditioned
by resulting qualities.

Each doing personality
experiences conditioning
that follows from its previous acts.

Accordingly, it's the enjoyer
of its past accomplishments,
as it is shaped through various forms
of seeming world that it perceives.

In every one of us, the doer
is the ruling principle
of life that journeys on through time *from*
by its own actions in the world. *5.7*

The individual self appears,
in every person, like the sun.

It shines by its own light, and thus
illuminates the seeming world.

As seen by virtue of the mind,
it gets associated with
false ego's pettiness of thought
and will and wishful fantasy.

As seen by virtue of itself,
it's like a point, dimensionless:
beyond all measure and compare, *from*
with nothing else beyond itself. *5.8*

The living principle of
personality may be perceived
as quite infinitesimal:

as always fine enough to be
completely present here within
whatever finite littleness
may be perceived by act of sense
or be conceived by act of mind.

And yet, from it arise
relationships and capabilities
extending to infinity, *from*
beyond all bounds of space and time. *5.9*

No gender qualifies its life.

It is not male. Nor is it female.
Nor has it some neuter gender
in between, describing it
as somehow lacking vital life.

But, through the personalities
superimposed on it by us,
it's what we cherish, what we care
for, what we watch and look for with *from*
concern, in those we come to love. *5.10*

Fooled by its own delusions of
imagination, feeling, sight,
the ego takes itself to be
a personality that has
been born and grows in many ways,
through nourishment that it receives.

But self, in truth, is quite impersonal:

as the unborn, unchanging
principle that's always here,
in everyone's experience,
within each personality.

As body journeys through the world,
self carries on through states of change:

and thus appears to be a 'soul',
successively assuming forms
of changing personality *from*
that follow on from previous acts. *5.11*

Seen through the changing attributes
of mind's and body's various acts,

it seems that the embodied self
takes on a great variety
of gross and subtle qualities
to form a personality.

But, seen through its inherent nature,
as the changeless, common centre
where all attributes are joined;

the self is known beyond all else, *from*
with nothing else beyond itself. *5.12*

Here, in the midst of a
chaotic-seeming world of birth and death,
it's unbegun and infinite:

as it appears to take on the
variety of changing forms
that seemingly condition it,
creating the appearances
of everything that seems perceived.

Thus it's the one reality *from*
containing all the universe. *5.13*

It's grasped only by being it:

by looking back into one's self,
from where sight comes, and thus returning
to one's own reality.

It is called 'bodiless'; for it
is not attached or limited
to any body in the world.

It is the source of love, from which
all doing and undoing comes.

It is the principle of light,
from which creation issues forth.

Whoever knows it leaves behind *from*
all petty personality. *5.14*

Immanent and transcendent [5]

Some speak of self-becoming nature,
or of passing time, as causing
all that happens in the world.

But seen more truly, all the
happenings of time and nature act
expressing unconditioned truth
in the conditioned things of world. *from 6.1*

This truth is all reality,
containing the entire world.

And further, it's pure consciousness:
the changeless source of changing time,
the unconditioned, knowing ground
of all conditioned qualities.

As moments pass, it carries on:
enabling different qualities
to be compared in course of time,
and lighting all that's ever known.

Inspired by the unseen guidance
of this unconditioned light,
all world's conditioned acts unfold.

It gets to be conceived as the
solidity of earth, as water's
changing flow, as fire's radiance,
air's conditioning, and as
the continuity of space
and time, pervading everywhere. *from 6.2*

[5]See *Interpreting the Upanishads*, pages 185-198, for an indication of how this retelling interprets the original text.

In everyone's experience,
the world is known through various acts
of mind and body: rising up
from underlying consciousness
to take attention out to world,
and then returning back again
to take in what is thus perceived.

Time and again, each person acts;
to learn a little of the world.

And every act ends in its source
of underlying consciousness,
as what was learned becomes absorbed.

Here, where all things are understood,
one comes through various partial truths
to unity of final truth, *from*
beneath all difference and change. *6.3*

It's from this common, changeless ground
that all conditioned acts arise.

It is from here that different
occurrences co-ordinate.

But here itself, there are no acts
and no occurrences at all.
Here, all that has been done by doing
is entirely destroyed.

At doing's end, the truth remains:
shown other than the changing world *from*
of seeming acts and happenings. *6.4*

It is the first, the unifying,
unmoved cause, of causes that
are moved to act towards results.

Thus it is seen beyond all time,
found undivided into parts;

the truth that has of old been heeded
as a worshipped God: who's
manifested in all forms, who is
the happening of all that has
become, and who stands here within, *from*
in everyone's own mind and heart. *6.5*

Seen through the tree of branching
happenings that form in time, the truth
is known as something else, beyond.

From it, the whole created world
goes out and then returns, and is
thus cycled and recycled round:
as different appearances
succeed each other in our minds.

The 'Lord' who's worshipped with devotion
cleanses sin, removes all ill,
brings order, justice, harmony.

Thus known, He's that in which all things
come home. He is that principle
abiding here in everyone: *from*
the self which does not change or die. *6.6*

That is the ultimate, great 'Lord
of Lords', the ultimate
divinity of all divinities,
the ultimate controlling principle
of all controlling powers.

It's that which must be known beyond:
as 'Lord' of the becoming world,
the principle that is invoked *from*
and worshipped through the name of 'God'. *6.7*

It has itself no faculty
of doing anything; nor has
it anything that it must do.

Nor is there anything that is
its equal or superior.

Nor is there even anything
that is additional to it.

As the *transcendent* source of all
of nature's energy, it is
revealed in many different ways.

For it is also *immanent*:
as the inherent principle
of nature shared in common by
all faculties that know the world,
all capabilities of strength *from*
and all the world's activities. *6.8*

It has no ruler or controller
anywhere, in all the world.

Not has it an exclusive sign
whose absence shows it is not there;
for it is present everywhere.

It is the underlying cause,
the common guiding principle,
of all our guiding faculties.

It has no further source of birth,
nor any guiding principle, *from*
found anywhere beyond itself. *6.9*

Just like a spider weaves a web
born forth of its own inner substance,

one sole principle of light
seems to surround itself with an
apparent universe that's made
of its own being, self-become.

To it, each one of us may turn,
from compromise with outward show,
to find all separateness dissolved *from*
in unobscured reality. *6.10*

This single principle of light,
pervading all the universe,
is hidden in all beings: as
the inner self in everyone.

It oversees all seeming acts:
as that which lives in everything,
observing all experiences,
itself completely unattached
to any kind of changing act.

Through all perceived appearances
of changing world, it is the witness: *from*
unconditioned, absolute. *6.11*

It's that one principle of
activating will, among the many
that aren't active in themselves.

And it's the underlying base
on which one seed of all creation
is made manifold, thus
giving rise to the variety
of things that happen in the world.

Whoever sees it standing here
through all experiences, as one's
own self, finds lasting happiness:

which can't be found in alien things *from*
that are not realized as self. *6.12*

It's the unchanging constancy
of constant things, the knowing core
of consciousness in conscious things,

the one reality among
the many seeming things of world,

the central principle of value
from which all desires arise.

And it's the underlying cause
of all phenomena: approached
through analytic reasoning,
or through techniques and disciplines *from*
that harness energy and power. *6.13*

The sun does not shine here, nor do
the moon and stars, nor lightning from
the sky, nor any alien fire.

It shines alone, by its own light.
Its very being is to shine.

All shines reflecting after it.
Whatever in the world appears
reflects its light of consciousness.

Thus all the world is nothing else
but the reflected light of self.

As self illuminates the world, *from*
it just illuminates itself. *6.14*

It is the one free spirit in
the midst of a conditioned world.

And it alone is all the fire
of energy that permeates
the changes and the transformations
of the world's conditioning.

Just knowing it takes one beyond
all seeming bonds, to deathlessness. *from*

There is no other way than this. *6.15*

It's the originating cause
of everything that's known and done;

the self-caused, knowing ground of learning
and of all conditioned qualities;

where all-destroying time
originates and is destroyed.

It's that which knows the primal field
of everyone's experience.
From that one guiding principle
comes order, meaning, quality.
All things are ruled by it, within.

It is the cause of bondage,
and of liberation from the cyclic
processes of birth and death. *from 6.16*

As deathless consciousness, pervading
everywhere, it is the changeless
witness of all happening.

It stands complete, as Lord and guardian
of this changing universe.

From it, all order and all
regularity originate.

There is no other cause of
ordered regularity, enabling
us to understand the world. *from 6.17*

In all that is perceived or thought
or felt within our changing minds,
it is that inner principle
of self-illuminating light:

which all creation must assume,
from which all learning is brought forth,
and for whose sake what's done takes place. *from 6.18*

It's always peaceful: undivided
into parts, and unaffected
by all action in the world.

It's free of blame, cannot be stained,
the final bridge of deathlessness:
just like a fire burning clean
to leave no smoke or ash behind. *from 6.19*

When humankind shall turn all space
back on itself, and shall thus roll
it up, just like an empty skin;

then there shall be an end to grief *from*
for the agnostic about 'God'. *6.20*

The highest secret of philosophy,
declared and handed down
from times long past, is not passed on
except to a disciple who *from*
thus finds true clarity and peace. *6.22*

Where love for truth transcends all else,
so too does love towards a teacher:

who is living truth itself,
for one to whom the truth is shown.

All meanings that are told and heard
shine forth from unconditioned light *from*
that is each person's real self. *6.23*

From the Rig Veda [1]

Creation [2]

Before conception has appeared,
no absence can arise at all;

for objects have not been conceived
that may be 'there' or be 'not there'.

Nor yet can qualities arise,
nor overarching principles
pervading different-seeming things;
for these too have not been conceived.

What is the base of consciousness
from which conception must arise,
before the world can be conceived?

Unmixed with seeming, doubtful things
that rise from mind's uncertainties,
what does pure consciousness contain?

Where can such consciousness be found?

Whose is this unmixed consciousness?

How does its knowledge carry on,
as things appear and disappear,
conceived by doubtful, changing mind?

[1]The Rig Veda is not of course an Upanishad. Instead, it is an earlier text. The retelling below is an interpretation of the 'Nāsadīya' passage: one of the philosophical 'hymns of creation' which occur in the late Rig Veda, showing a transition of thought from the mythical imagination of the Vedas to the more abstract philosophy of the Upanishads.

[2]See *Interpreting the Upanishads*, pages 52-59, for an indication of how this retelling interprets the original text.

Just what provides stability,
security and certainty,
as consciousness continues on:

through seeming things that come and go,
appearing when they are perceived
and disappearing when they're not?

Through changing mind's apparent waves
of form and name and quality,

what really is the consciousness
of which each seeming wave consists, *from*
just like the boundless depths below? *10.129.1*

Before conception rises up
from unconditioned consciousness,
there is no change nor difference;
for time and space aren't yet conceived.

With nothing born, there is no death
and so there can't be deathlessness.

Since world has not yet been conceived,
there's nothing that appears by day
or disappears again at night.

No world appears as we awake,
nor disappears when we're asleep.

There is no night. There is no day.
There is no waking state, nor sleep.

Within the world that mind conceives,
our bodies live by breathing air.
So too, our minds breathe meaning out
through words and acts, and breathe back in
perceptions from an outer world.

But consciousness is life itself,
which lives by its inherent light
that lights itself, without the need
for any breathing out or in.

In truth, as known by consciousness,
what seems outside is known within.

There really is no outside world
that's separate from some inner mind.
There's no outside and no inside. *from 10.129.2*

When mind looks down to its own depths
from where conception seems to rise,
a blinding darkness first appears
concealed in its own ignorance.

Here, all seems primal, inchoate:
with unseen powers surging up
from depths of dark obscurity.

From this uncertain, shifting base,
whatever truth may be conceived
comes dressed in empty vanity:

of mind that's driven blindly on
by energies and powers of will
it doesn't fully understand. *from 10.129.3*

Desire turns on consciousness
right from the start of seeming life:
where mind is seeded by desire
to form a stream of changing thoughts
by which the world is then conceived.

When thought turns back to heart within,
to clarify obscurities
and search for undistorted truth,

at first there seems blank nothingness
where everything has disappeared.

What is this seeming nothingness?

It is the absence of apparent
things, not of reality.

In it, all seeming thought dissolves
and what remains is consciousness,
unmixed with any seeming thing.

As thought dissolves, pure consciousness
shines out as all reality:

where different-seeming things are joined *from*
as mere appearances of one. *10.129.4*

Unseen by body, sense or mind,
the light of consciousness extends
through all the universe it shows:

through everything that seems to be
or not to be, through space and time,
through every state of changing mind.

Where mind completely disappears,
as in the peace of dreamless sleep,
there comes a state that mind conceives
as dark and empty nothingness.

But nothingness cannot seem dark
unless it's known by consciousness:
whose light shines unconditioned here,
unseen by body, sense and mind.

Back in the world that mind conceives,
just where can consciousness be found?

Is it beneath appearances?
Is it above what mind desires?

Is it the subtle seeds of mind
from which creation is conceived?
Is it the energies and powers
that shape the world and get things done?

Is it the underlying power
that moves creation from the start?
Is it the drive that follows on *from*
to look for better life beyond? *10.129.5*

Who really knows? Just what is it
in each of us that knows the things
our minds conceive and senses see?

Just who or what in us can tell
from where appearances are born,
from where creation is conceived?

Our faculties of mind and sense
are part of the created world.
They cannot therefore come before
this world has been conceived by mind.

What then is prior to the mind?

Just who or what in us can know
from where conception rises up *from*
to form the world we think we see? *10.129.6*

From where does seeming world arise?

Does it in truth arise at all,
or does it only *seem* to rise
from incorrect appearances
mistakenly perceived by mind?

The changing things of seeming world,
and their conception in our minds,
are known by changeless consciousness:
which carries on, while seeming things
and mind's conceptions come and go.

In everyone's experience,
as feelings, thoughts, perceptions and
their seeming objects come and go,

pure consciousness alone remains:
continuing through time and change,
to know all these appearances.

It's only from this final base,
of unconditioned consciousness,
that world's conception can be known; *from*
if it is truly known at all. *10.129.7*

Index

www.ingramcontent.com/pod-product-compliance
Ingram Content Group UK Ltd.
Pitfield, Milton Keynes, MK11 3LW, UK
UKHW021706190726
13853UKWH00001B/440

9 788188 071494